Editor-in-Chief and Founder:
  Lyndon H. LaRouche, Jr.
Editorial Board: *Lyndon H. LaRouche, Jr. , Helga Zepp-LaRouche, Robert Ingraham, Tony Papert, Gerald Rose, Dennis Small, Jeffrey Steinberg, William Wertz*
Co-Editors: *Robert Ingraham, Tony Papert*
Managing Editor: *Nancy Spannaus*
Technology: *Marsha Freeman*
Books: *Katherine Notley*
Ebooks: *Richard Burden*
Graphics: *Alan Yue*
Photos: *Stuart Lewis*
Circulation Manager: *Stanley Ezrol*

INTELLIGENCE DIRECTORS
Counterintelligence: *Jeffrey Steinberg, Michele Steinberg*
Economics: *John Hoefle, Marcia Merry Baker, Paul Gallagher*
History: *Anton Chaitkin*
Ibero-America: *Dennis Small*
Russia and Eastern Europe: *Rachel Douglas*
United States: *Debra Freeman*

INTERNATIONAL BUREAUS
Bogotá: *Miriam Redondo*
Berlin: *Rainer Apel*
Copenhagen: *Tom Gillesberg*
Houston: *Harley Schlanger*
Lima: *Sara Madueño*
Melbourne: *Robert Barwick*
Mexico City: *Gerardo Castilleja Chávez*
New Delhi: *Ramtanu Maitra*
Paris: *Christine Bierre*
Stockholm: *Ulf Sandmark*
United Nations, N.Y.C.: *Leni Rubinstein*
Washington, D.C.: *William Jones*
Wiesbaden: *Göran Haglund*

ON THE WEB
e-mail: eirns@larouchepub.com
www.larouchepub.com
www.executiveintelligencereview.com
www.larouchepub.com/eiw
Webmaster: *John Sigerson*
Assistant Webmaster: *George Hollis*
Editor, Arabic-language edition: *Hussein Askary*

EIR (ISSN 0273-6314) *is published weekly (50 issues), by EIR News Service, Inc., P.O. Box 17390, Washington, D.C. 20041-0390. (703) 777-9451*

European Headquarters: E.I.R. GmbH, Postfach Bahnstrasse 9a, D-65205, Wiesbaden, Germany
Tel: 49-611-73650
Homepage: http://www.eirna.com
e-mail: eirna@eirna.com
Director: Georg Neudecker

Montreal, Canada: 514-461-1557

Denmark: EIR - Danmark, Sankt Knuds Vej 11, basement left, DK-1903 Frederiksberg, Denmark. Tel.: +45 35 43 60 40, Fax: +45 35 43 87 57. e-mail: eirdk@hotmail.com.

Mexico City: EIR, Sor Juana Inés de la Cruz 242-2 Col. Agricultura C.P. 11360 Delegación M. Hidalgo, México D.F. Tel. (5525) 5318-2301 eirmexico@gmail.com

Postmaster: Send all address changes to *EIR*, P.O. Box 17390, Washington, D.C. 20041-0390.

Signed articles in *EIR* represent the views of the authors, and not necessarily those of the Editorial Board.

The Far Side of the Moon or Bust

Nothing Can Succeed without The Discovery of the Principle of The Back Side of the Moon

March 3—What are nations? Why do we have them? What are they for? In reality, their purpose is nothing other than to better the condition of humanity, as John F. Kennedy said when he announced the mission to send a man to the Moon and return him safely to Earth, by the end of the long-ago 1960s. The means for that advancement of the human condition,— it is both the end and the means at once,— is through genuine discovery or noësis. What is true for a nation, is even truer for an alliance of nations like the BRICS, the Eurasian Economic Union, or the Shanghai Cooperation Organization. Even if they are still new and fragile, these linkups of Eurasian nations already point to the future of humanity.

Only in this condition of creativity is man truly happy; only in this condition is he genuinely himself. Yet this condition is virtually outlawed in the United States of today and recent times, as in Europe, and in Central and South America. Peer-group pressure and all the traditions of education insist on mere repetition of the approved formulas; on mere deduction rather than noësis. Under this regimen man can never know the future.

Just now, at this moment, the remarkable and unexpected success of Russian President Putin's intervention into Barack Obama's and Hillary Clinton's murderous stew in Syria, has forced to the surface the realization that trans-Atlantic society has been a failure,— a historic failure. We must look to Eurasia, and the United States must henceforth have a Pacific, rather than Atlantic orientation.

Obama shows forth clearly as a British agent, and nothing but a British agent, who has killed a great many people. And Hillary Clinton is in the same mold.

The trans-Atlantic community is a lost cause right now; it can't and won't come back in this form. If it is to come back, it will first have to be reborn anew. The remains of the trans-Atlantic community, in this form, are gone. We must create a new form of society, as has been done in the past,— by Charlemagne, for example. That's what we have to fight for: a future which will be a true future.

This is the meaning of Kesha Rogers' highly intellectual and highly inspirational campaign to return to our future in the exploration and conquest of Solar and Galactic space. Key individuals are already being drawn towards Kesha from around the country and the world.

What this means is what Lyndon LaRouche said in a discussion on March 1.

We've got to say one thing. One thing: nothing will be successful unless the nations recognize the discovery of the principle of the back side of the Moon. In other words, you can't say you can take what's going on right now, and interpret that into a good effect. You've got to cancel that, and say, "Well, the problem is we have not yet understood what lies behind the Moon." And when we find out what is behind the Moon, which is being worked on by the Chinese and other persons, and going back to the ABCs of the original space program, without going back to these things which Obama cut down,— Obama struck those programs down, and therefore he should be punished seriously for his crimes on that account. Instead of trying to interpret something and put a different, better spin on it,— that doesn't work. Because without the space program, which means the back side of the Moon in particular,— without that approach, you don't get anything, you don't get anywhere. You've got to do that! It's not an option that you might choose or not choose. You can't deny it: You have to recognize that that's what you have to do.

EIR Contents

www.larouchepub.com Volume 43, Number 11, March 11, 2016

China Daily

Cover This Week

Chinese astronaut Wang Yaping teaching a class in Space physics live from orbit to 60 million students, including these Beijing high school students, during a June 2013 Space mission.

I. The Revival of the Space Program

The View from Texas To the Far Side of the Moon

March 5—Megan Beets of the LaRouche PAC Science Team gave this report to the March 4 International LaRouche PAC Webcast.

I can tell you from my visit to Texas that at this moment, when the breakdown of the trans-Atlantic system is undeniable—we're witnessing the complete malfunctioning and shutdown of this old system— we're also seeing the reopening of the space program down in Texas.

Now the event that I was privileged to participate in with Kesha Rogers and Tom Wysmuller in Texas, represents a real beginning of a change of direction of the United States, a rebirth, so to speak, of the United States as a nation. Now, the requirement today is that the United States dump our commitment, our addiction, to this dead, dying trans-Atlantic system, and decide once again to take up a mission in the sense of purpose and contribution to mankind.

Now, you look around today. You look around at our citizens. You look at the heroin epidemic. You look at the death, the self-induced deaths from drugs, from suicide, from alcoholism. You look at the breakdown in cities like Flint, Michigan, the breakdown in places like certain counties of West Virginia that were once booming coal towns. There's no reflection in the United States of reality.

Ian Overton

Speaking on the March 4 LaRouche PAC webcast, Megan Beets reported the necessity of a renewed Space program to restore the sense of purpose to the United States. China's leadership in Space is providing progress for humanity. Beets was a participant at the conference to revive the U.S. Space program, held near the Johnson Space Center.

Now, what's reality? Look at the leadership coming from Asia, particularly from China. Look at the kinds of optimistic developments, the progress for humanity, that's coming from the leadership of China and their space program, and in their commitment to development projects which are beginning to take hold and take place all across Eurasia. That's reality. There's no reflection of this yet inside the United States.

And so, when we look around, it's not just that the U.S. economy has disappeared. The United States has disappeared. There's no sense of a unified purpose. There's no sense of a unified mission for the existence of the United States as a nation, and there's no sense within our people of what *we*, as a nation, will organize ourselves to contribute to the purposes of mankind.

Now you contrast that with the U.S. sense of purpose and mission under John F. Kennedy and his Presidency, and his leadership within the United States, and his dedication to the space program. Now, as anyone who truthfully remembers— and most especially, those people who were directly involved—can tell you, this wasn't just a mission for the United States. This was a real mission for all of mankind. And this was reflected in some anecdotes at the Texas event last Saturday from some of the participants who themselves were engineers or otherwise employed in NASA during the Apollo missions.

In an anecdote, Tom Wysmuller said that he had disagreed with Wernher von Braun's view that we should be sharing some of our technology with the Russians, and his mind was changed by von Braun. There was another former NASA employee who said that at first, in the 1990s, he disagreed with President Clinton's sharing of U.S. space technology with the former Soviet Union—with Russia. But he said that once he started working with Russian engineers, he realized that our mission is mankind; it's unified; it's the same. And this was reflected throughout the entire event: the sense that our work during the space program was contributing fundamental developments and contributions, not to the progress of the United States, but to the progress of man as a whole.

Now, why? What is the space program? What happened during the space program in the United States?

Well, not only was the common, the general citizen transformed. Not only were there innumerable and immeasurable benefits from the economic spin-offs. But most importantly, the people were transformed. The astronauts were fundamentally transformed. The engineers working in the space program were fundamentally transformed, as we confronted problems in space, problems that forced us to overturn our assumptions about the principles which govern and control the Universe. And each of these problems that we confronted, we were to conquer. And you see that in the accounts of the people who were involved during that time in the space program: that we were able to pull together around a common mission, thousands and thousands of people across the country to confront these challenges in our knowledge about the Universe, and to conquer them.

And in that way, in a very short period of time, man began to rapidly transform himself and change to be a more powerful species. We began to progress into a species with more power and control over the processes in the Universe, to the point that we were able to land people on the surface of the Moon, which fundamentally transformed our ideas and our knowledge of what the Moon itself is, of what potential the Moon holds for a new platform of development for man, which was completely unknown until the accomplishments of Apollo.

Now this is what the Chinese are doing today with their space program. In 2018, just two years from now, the Chinese plan to land on the far side of the Moon. This has never been done before. The far side of the Moon has been imaged with satellites; it's been seen by the human eyes of the American astronauts who orbited the Moon. But nobody has ever landed on the far side of the Moon.

Now, people may say, "Well, we know what the Moon is; we've looked at it. We've taken pictures." But the fact is, the far side of the Moon is a completely unknown quantity to us. When we land there, for example, what do we think the far side can teach us? When we land there, we'll have a chance to confront our fundamental notions about the formation of the Moon, the formation of the Earth, and possibly other planets in the Solar system, with the unique geological investigations that we'll be able to perform there.

When we land there, and when we're able to set up astronomical observatories in the very low radio frequency range, which is a band of the electromagnetic spectrum in which it is impossible to look at the Solar system from anywhere attainable to us besides the far side of the Moon; when we are able to look at the Solar system in this new range, we're very likely going to discover that the planets, the interstellar medium, distant galaxies, different stars, could exhibit processes to us which were completely invisible before.

It's this kind of potential for mankind to transform our powers, to transform our relationship to the Solar system itself, that's being offered by the Chinese actions today. And it's this sense of meaning, this sense of mobilization and commitment to progress for all of mankind, which is what we, in Texas, are reminding people of. It's what Kesha is reminding people of— even people who participated in these great accomplishments 40 or 50 years ago, and who might have encountered now a sense of demoralization with the actions since that time. We're drawing people out, back to a commitment to this mission. And Kesha is showing once again that the United States can, and must, commit itself to this kind of purpose for all of mankind.

In these beginnings that we are seeing in Texas, we find that people there still associate themselves with reality, and are now playing a leading role, with Kesha, in promoting the understanding that this mission for mankind is the viable option for the United States.

There Are *No* Limits to Growth: Mankind Must Conquer Space!

by Ian Overton

March 1—On Saturday, Feb. 27, 2016, at a conference held in League City, Texas, LaRouche PAC Policy Committee leader Kesha Rogers demonstrated to the people of Texas, and to the rest of United States, the quality of thinking and the quality of fight required to move America into the future.

Under the theme, "There Are *No* Limits to Growth: Mankind Must Conquer Space,"[1] an all day conference was held in the shadow of the Johnson Space Center under the auspices of the Schiller Institute. Rogers, who keynoted the event, was joined for a panel discussion by Tom Wysmuller, a member of the NASA Alumni Association and The Right Climate Stuff group, and Megan Beets of the LaRouche PAC Science Team.

In both 2010 and 2012, Rogers ran campaigns for U.S. Congress from the district representing the Johnson Space Center. She won the Democratic Party nomination in both races, campaigning under the slogan, "Save NASA, Impeach Obama."

Ian Overton

Discussion continues after the Schiller Institute's conference on the Extraterrestrial Imperative, held near the Johnson Space Center, Texas. Kesha Rogers is second from right. Megan Beets and Tom Wysmuller are facing the camera.

The courage and leadership that Rogers demonstrated in those races were apparent again at the League City event, where a lively discussion and dialogue took place between audience members and the speakers. This included useful insights by members of an audience which included NASA alumni and contractors, and other science-minded individuals, into how their own thinking had been challenged, and the way in which they had come to re-evaluate some of their own "fixed" beliefs.

---

1. The event was broadcast live on the Internet and the archive video is here.

FIGURE 1

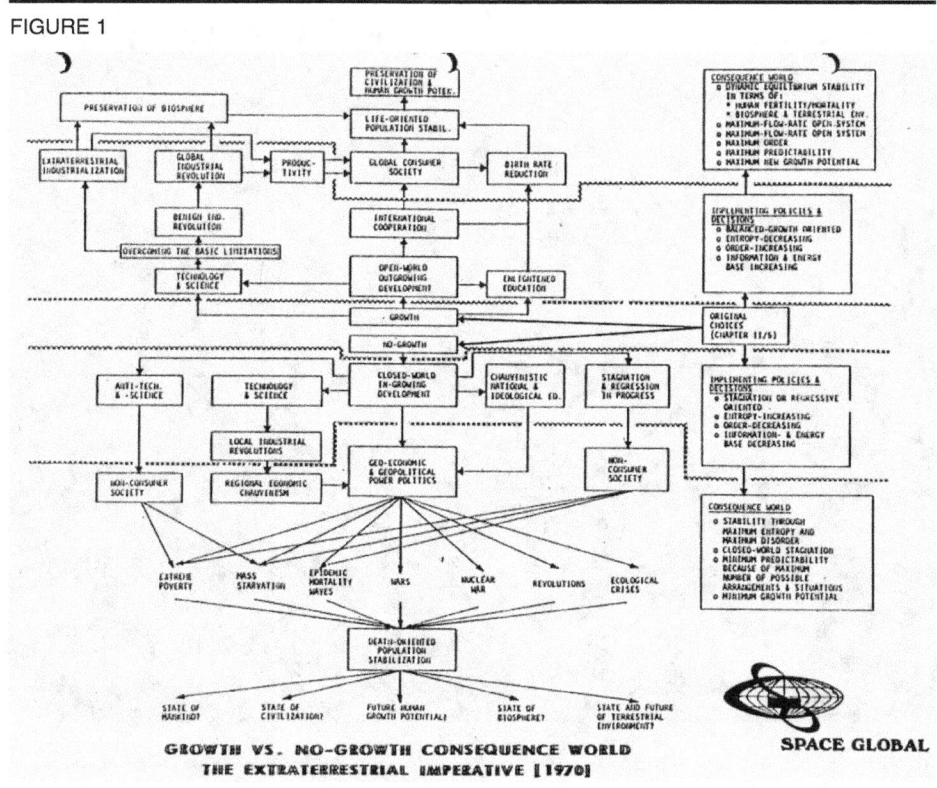

**GROWTH VS. NO-GROWTH CONSEQUENCE WORLD
THE EXTRATERRESTRIAL IMPERATIVE [1970]**

SPACE GLOBAL

Space Global/Krafft Ehricke

Krafft Ehricke's flowchart illustrates the necessary physical consequences of the choice between a paradigm of life and growth, and a no-growth paradigm of war, famine, disease, and death.

Inaugurating the Age of Reason

"The question facing NASA," began Rogers, "is not why was this or that program was cut, but why is our extra-terrestrial imperative—which Krafft Ehricke defined as the true nature and basis of mankind's creative existence—being attacked? How do we restore this identity; how do we remove the limitations that have been placed on our imagination?"

To begin answering this question, Rogers quoted German space pioneer Krafft Ehricke himself, who said, "The world of modern industrial man is no more closed within the biosphere than it is flat. Human growth hinges on technology and its translation into industry.... The one underlying, unambiguous technology [that accomplishes this] is space technology." Ehricke illustrated this choice between a growth paradigm of life and a no-growth paradigm of war, famine, disease, and death, in a flow chart demonstrating the necessary physical consequences of our daily choice of accepting one policy over the other (see **Figure 1**).

Society has lost its capacity to reason as true human beings, because the mission of the space program, and what it truly represents, has been taken away. The ability to create our future has been taken away, and the population has been reduced to the mental status of beasts. Thus, the purpose of this event was to unleash a new paradigm—The Age of Reason—where these limitations have been removed, and mankind is free to realize our destiny as mankind in the universe, and shed the last cultural residues of bestiality.

Wysmuller: Science Driver's Systemic Effects

Following these opening remarks, Tom Wysmuller described how his work at NASA during the early 1970s—as one of nine people picked to be "executive interns" who would eventually replace other executives—uniquely provided him a top-down view of how NASA's space technology contributed to Ehricke's Growth Paradigm. Wysmuller presented a detailed overview of the cascade of technologies generated by our space endeavors, pointing out that nearly every job in the United States has been improved through our past science drivers—even that of the proverbial ditch-digger, who now uses a titanium-enhanced shovel blade and GPS to determine his dig zone.

"This kind of technological advancement should not be put at the whim of political opinions!" Wysmuller exclaimed. "If we had a Mars program, we would dramatically increase these technologies, we would give people on Earth a *raison d'être.*"

In discussing Mars colonization preceded by lunar industrialization, as the next giant leaps for human progress, Wysmuller repeatedly emphasized the need for global collaboration among the four major space powers—the United States, Europe, Russia, and China—and told the audience how he was personally corrected in his thinking on this matter by Wernher von Braun.

"At the time," Wysmuller stated, "I opposed sharing docking technologies with Russia for the Soyuz mission. I did not see why we should give away our superior technology to our opponents. But I was wrong. Von Braun convinced me of this when he said, 'Tom, if any of our astronauts happened to be in trouble, and the Russians actually had a bird on the launch pad they could send up, all they would be able to do is look out the window and wave as they passed by. They wouldn't be able to rescue us; we could not be rescued, and we would not be able to rescue them.'"

The mutually beneficial win-win optimism of America's two godfathers of space flight, Krafft Ehricke and Werner von Braun, struck a deep chord within the audience, and Wysmuller challenged his colleagues to rethink their current fear of collaboration with China and Russia, in light of what could be accomplished for mankind by such cooperation.

China Daily

Wang Yaping teaches a class in space physics live from orbit to 60 million school children during the June 2013 Shenzhou 10 mission. Here, a small part of her audience at a Beijing high school.

Beets: Political Mobilization—and Demobilization

Picking up on this theme, Megan Beets briefly described how Lyndon LaRouche developed this perspective of a win-win growth paradigm as the science of physical economy. Nations are able to collaborate and grow by making conscious, willful decisions, not simply by trial and error. Such a policy program has been officially adopted by China and Russia, as typified by the trajectory for growth that China has put into its space program as part of its One Belt, One Road policy with the BRICS group of nations and others. To survive, the United States must reject the willful and arrogant take-down of its "go it alone" manned space program by Obama, and join with China and Russia in realizing the common aims of all mankind.

A few months after China launched its first astronaut into space, in 2004, President Bush announced that the United States would return to the Moon, as a launch pad for getting to Mars. NASA laid out a detailed plan for getting back to the Moon by 2015, and to Mars by 2030.

"In reading this report," Beets told the audience, "I was struck by how everything NASA had been doing was now being reorganized under a single mission. Even projects like New Horizons, which were begun years earlier, were reinterpreted to be part of this unified focus. NASA began to mobilize and regain what was lost after Apollo was cancelled." The new Aries-1 and Aries-5 rocket launch systems, the Altair lunar lander, the Constellation vehicle, and the Orion crew capsule were developed with 50 years of science and engineering improvements to build upon,— yet the Obama Administration's FY2011 budget cancelled all of this, declaring it over budget, behind schedule, and "lacking innovation."

"Yet more crucial than the specifics of China's mission objectives," Beets concluded, "is the creation and development of mankind. That's the ultimate mission. That's why, despite the attack on our space program, a record 18,300 Americans have applied to NASA to become astronauts, more than triple the number of applications received in 2012. Whether it's conscious or not, science is not a matter of tripping over a new fact, like a squirrel collecting nuts. As mankind makes discoveries of the universe, we redefine the universe, and that power is what we have to instill consciously into the people of the U.S.A. today. That will create the political victory for the Age of Reason."

Audience Transformed

The audience of NASA alumni and contractors, teachers, and engineers responded enthusiastically to this challenge of the win-win strategy of the Age of Reason—so much so that one organizer noted that if this momentum keeps up, we may have to rename League City and call it Manhattan, Texas!

A rocket scientist spoke up, attacking the opportunistic politicians of our country. He said he is inspired by the idea of Helium-3, but is afraid of the Chinese as well. Kesha Rogers challenged him by showing that the source of the problem with our politicians is the corrupting influence of Wall Street, and Tom Wysmuller reminded him that the Chinese have repeatedly offered us a hand of cooperation on these ventures, yet these same politicians are the ones forcing them to go it alone. Later, that rocket scientist was to admit that he now had come to understand how his fears had been generated, and that he had to change the way he had been thinking.

A Chinese-American photovoltaic engineer asked the panelists to explain the root cause of the United States' shutdown, since it is clearly not any lack of enthusiasm in the population. Megan Beets drove home the point just made about Wall Street. The cancellation of the Apollo Program occurred under President Nixon, a crony for Wall Street speculators, right after he destroyed the fixed exchange rate financial system. We are currently living with the effects of 40 years under a no-growth paradigm. People must recognize this, in order to stop being confused about why good projects are not allowed to happen.

A contractor for NASA spoke against the way in which the scientific community tries to adapt to this "practical" budget-cutting mentality, by attacking the way the James Webb Space Telescope is being promoted. "People are talking as if it's OK that the Hubble

---

Highlights of China's Space Program

• **2003:** Shenzhou 5 launched first Chinese citizen into space a few months before the United States announced its return to the Moon.

• **2004:** China began lunar program, the dream of of space pioneer Ouyang Ziyuan.

• **2007:** China launched Chang'e-1, mapped Moon in 3D, made a mineral map. Ten thousand Chinese students interviewed; 99% were closely following the space program, 90% believed they will travel to the Moon one day.

• **2008:** Shenzhou 7 first space walk, broadcast live.

• **2012:** First phase of Chinese space station, then auto and manual docking with crew.

• **2013:** Second crew rendezvoused with space station. Astronaut Wang Yaping gave a physics class to 60 million Chinese school children from orbit.

• **2013-14:** Chang'e-3 soft landing on Moon, the first since 1976. Yutu Rover imaged Earth with ultraviolet telescope.

• **2014:** Chang'e 5-T1 orbits the Moon, images the far side, and tests atmospheric reentry technology on its return to Earth.

• **2017:** Mission to return soil sample from lunar surface.

• **2018:** Plan to land on far side of Moon, establish very low frequency (VLF) radio telescope and He-3 mining operations.

• **Early 2020s:** Expect to finish space station. China wants it to be an international effort and has invited participation of the United States and other space-faring countries, and also those without space capability.

Space Telescope and the International Space Station are being decommissioned, and being allowed to burn up in the atmosphere. It's not OK!" she exclaimed. "James Webb is not a replacement for Hubble because it sees in a different wavelength! They are complements, not substitutes. But it's being sold this way because the money isn't budgeted to keep them active. The problem is not their usefulness, it's the way people think about money, as more important than science."

A NASA alum who developed stabilization technology for re-entry vehicles gave personal testimony in support of what the panelists had been saying about the need to dispel the mask of fear used by those who would keep us from working together. "I opposed President Clinton's decision to jointly build the International Space Station with the Russians, because of my experiences

Jin Liwang/Xinhua

A younger component of Wang Yaping's "classroom" of 60 million across 80,000 schools, during her live presentation from Earth orbit. President Xi told the crew that the mission "carries the space dream of the Chinese nation" and will "show the Chinese passion to reach for the stars."

growing up in the Cold War of the 1950s," he said. "But my experience of working with Russians on the structural integrity of ISS changed me.

"I met them, we ate dinner together, and I got to know them personally. I discovered that neither of us liked our leaders' reactions, but we shared ideas as engineers and scientific minds. I've come to see that the cooperation approach is more important than 'Us First.'"

Other participants asked how to get more people to understand the importance of NASA's accomplishments and how to get these scientists to stop being cynical about politicians and budgets, but instead exert their authority as scientists to make policy for mankind's future. Rogers responded that this is precisely why she ran her campaigns for U.S. Congress and her 2014 campaign for U.S. Senate. "Scientists were surprised I came to their events," she said. "But I told them, NASA is not just some country club, it is the nation's organization, our science driver. We deserve for NASA to be able to organize the nation around the success we could be achieving."

This provoked Wysmuller to call for a series of international brain trust conferences. "I am going to China soon, and I plan to help this along. We need free and open discussions to dispel prejudices. We have a world here. We need to work together. When the barriers get broken, everybody wins."

II. The Collapse of the Trans-Atlantic Region

Mankind Has a Destiny in the Stars

March 6—The following are edited excerpts from the *LaRouche PAC Fireside Chat with Lyndon LaRouche of March 3.*

LaRouche: I would say the issue is that despite, on the one side, what some of the leading candidates think about themselves,— which is usually foolishness, of course, chiefly,— but there's something going on in the United States, and it's going to develop, evolve into a new form. In other words what the leading candidates will attempt to do, the so-called leading candidates,— they will fail. Because what they will present will be incredible to the average citizen in the United States.

Question: I used to organize with you guys in the '90s, and it was one of the most peaceful and joyful times of my life. The situation now is, I have to work every day to try to maintain a lifestyle and family and everything like that. But my question would be, how would we reconcile the conflict between day-to-day survival and actually being the citizens that we should be, propagating this new era for mankind?

LaRouche: What you have to do, the obvious thing is, you have to change the agenda. That means that Obama has to be cleaned out, because Obama is one of your major objects. As long as Obama's in charge, you don't have a chance. So therefore, if we can break Obama, and bring other factors into place,— and this is possible, this is not something just out of the blue. The point is, is the citizens of the United States, if they are mobilized and they are saying, "Look, we're not going to sit here and die,"— and essentially for many people

NASA/Jim Grossmann

All the presidential candidates are expendable, pieces of trash, LaRouche said. But "you shouldn't be pessimistic," because the effort to go back to a Space program is a policy change that could turn over the rigged political game. Here, Space Shuttle Endeavour lifts off on July 15, 2009.

it's just that: They're sitting there and dying. Let's take people for example, who are sick, who are weak, who have been depleted, and they are simply dying. They're dying of self-inflicted wounds, because they are totally demoralized, and the main thing we have to do is to bring our citizens in the United States into a sense of responsibility and authority for changing the course of behavior throughout the population. For example, most people in the United States, who are working people, so-called, that category,— they are dying. They are dying by self-inflicted wounds, by desperation, and they're accepting death, and this is wrong!

So the main thing we have to do, is concentrate on the fact,— you have to look at your neighbor. Your neighbors may be on the way to killing themselves by suicide. So therefore you've got to get this citizen, who is ready to go to death because of depression and all these kinds of things of the circumstances of their life,— you've got to get them to fight back, for life. And if you can get people to fight back for life, we can win.

Question: [from the Internet] This is a gentleman who is a former state representative from Maine, who participated in a conference on the Silk Road with you back in the 1990s. He's asking in reference to Helga's speech in India this week:

"It's so fitting that she is there with all the leaders. She has worked tirelessly for decades on this." He says when he got involved in the New Silk Road, he then traveled to Asia, and that helped him understand the international development proposal and "what is needed to quantum-leap us away from war, and instead have peace through mutual international development. Swords and Guns into Starships and Shovels. Lyn, I would like to hear your comments and assessments of the importance of what your wife Helga is involved in."

LaRouche: Well, what both Helga and I have been concentrated on for a long period of time, but I'm an old geezer and, therefore I am required to pay attention to things that I wish I didn't have to pay any attention to, but my commitments are the same as hers. She's just more effective now, because of her life, you know, she's young, and she therefore is able to do more things than I am able to do.

I'm very efficient actually, in terms of dealing with the major questions that I have to deal with. I deal with these several times each week, and I do deal with that. But Helga's position is such, and her skills and her ability to move around throughout the planet, gives her an

advantage, and that's what she's doing. She's just done that, in terms of this process that she's now going to complete—her travel for that purpose at this time.

And she is a very creative person. She has very qualified measures. She has a lot of experience in all of these matters and she's a leading figure in dealing with these matters. So that's where it stands, and she's doing the job and she will be manifesting her next level of achievement which will be coming in, in the next several days.

We Can Topple the Whole Thing

Question: I was watching today the show being put on by Romney and Trump, and although the clowns were on and they are not the answer, obviously, something that Trump is doing, the reason that he is performing so successfully in the Republican primary, is that he has tapped into the frustration and the feelings of the working class, and the fact that the working class has been undergoing this mass destruction. And I don't think he fully realizes why, but he knows this is happening, and he's tapped into it. And the establishment in the Republican Party is unable to accept that he has gotten this picture in his mind of what's happening to the ordinary person. And it's accurate to a certain extent. The Republican establishment just cannot get it into their heads how bad off people are, and this is what has been happening. And this is why I feel that although Trump is not the answer, he may wind up as President!

LaRouche: Well, I would say I wouldn't even think in those terms. The problem is this man is useless. He's a disgusting person, intrinsically disgusting. He has no merits whatsoever. He's just a tool used by certain agencies.

Now, I know his history pretty well, and I can tell you, his history as I know it very well, is a piece of junk. There's nothing really of content to it. It is simply a staged operation, under the influence of certain parts of the government who are playing games! There is no reality.

I mean, the whole thing, Hillary, him, so forth, they're all expendable. She's expendable. Look what she is! Look, she is a murderer. She made herself a murderer for Obama! And that's what she did, and the thing is on the record. Obama was the director of this thing. She joined it, she went along with it. She became ambitious. She sold her soul out for who knows what, but she sold her soul out. That's what she did.

Now, the whole thing is a piece of trash. With a very small movement on the part of some within the body of the people of the United States, the citizens, we could topple this whole damned thing and get rid of it, within a very quick time. The anger factor which is built up there, ready to tip everything over, can happen. My commitment is, let's topple the whole thing. Let's turn it all over, let's shut it down. We can start all over again. And that can be done by the United States. It doesn't take the majority of the people of the United States to do that. All you have to do is have enough people for that.

I know about that, in point of fact. If people of skill, that is economic skill, are operating in various parts of the United States, I know that many of them are on the edge of thinking about turning everything over. Now, that may not happen, but it could happen, very likely. And the best bet you can get at these prices, is to go to turn everything over. Just turn it over!

For example, we've had a change in terms of policy. What happened recently is we went back to the space program. It was done in Texas, under the leadership of a person associated with me. We went to work on it. We are extending that influence into California and so forth. We are going back to the space program! We are very serious about it, and we think we can make quite a bit of a to-do on this thing.

So you shouldn't be pessimistic. Realize that these guys are a bunch of bums,— you wish you had never met them before or anything like that. But!—if we pull ourselves together, we may be able to just turn everything over. Because what is being offered to the people in the United States is nothing! It's worthless! It's crap! All we need is enough to get something started, where people will mobilize themselves to create an actually active form of the United States, as an operating institution.

Question: [from the Internet] I have another question. This comes from an activist with LaRouche PAC, asking: "How can an arch-criminal like Hillary Clinton even become a Presidential candidate in the United States?"

LaRouche: It could be a very slight change, in commitment in direction, can change everything overnight.

Now, what overnight means is something we have to examine, but I know it can be done overnight, because all the evidence which I do have as evidence proves that. All it takes is one twist in the right direction, and Hillary is finished.

[In response to a follow-up question on the *New York Times* exposé of Hillary]—Don't say just the *New York Times,* because this is an off-and-on factor. It was a factor inside the *New York Times,* which decided to do that. What they did was the truth, it was not the full truth, but it was a pretty good truth, and if you read it carefully, she's out! Now, she has not been dumped out, yet. But she's eligible to be dumped out at any time that things just turn in the right direction, and she is gone.

It's Very Fragile

Question: I'm wondering about the Secretary of State John Kerry because it seems like he has actually been doing his job to some extent. I mean, he's actually been—it's some good diplomacy.

LaRouche: Yeah, that's kind of too narrow, though. The fact of the matter is, inside the United States, among people who are influential inside the processes of the United States, there are different kinds of moves and shifts in the process of the action.

Now, what you're getting always in this thing, you're getting some elements of informed popular opinion who will actually recognize what the problem is and what to do to change it. They will bring things, if not to tip over everything that should be tipped over, but they will be at the point of tipping things over.

Now our job, and my job and your job, is to recognize that fact: What we have to do, is we have to tip everything over. And it only takes a limited number of people to assemble themselves, and to say, "we're going to kick the thing over." And that's all it takes.

This thing is very fragile. You have a population in the United States which has no comprehension of what reality is. Only a limited number of people in the United States have any competent understanding of what the situation is in the United States. Most people in the United States have no comprehension whatsoever, of what the truth is about the situation in the United States. A few of us, me included, know what this is about. But we are limited by the fact that most people are so scared, so disoriented, that they don't see reality! And the minute that any of us who do know what this is all about get a chance to make the case, we will make the case! And it will be very easy to get rid of people like Obama, to get rid of people like Trump, or Thump or whatever he is, and people like that. They can be toppled immediately. They're vulnerable, they're cheap shots. They are not real!

And so therefore, those of us who may be a limited number of people, in terms of countable heads in this,— where I'm sitting, we have the hands which with a twist of the wrist, can turn things around!

Question: I have one report from a contact that I spoke with not an hour and a half ago, and then I have a question. The quick report is from an old contact who in the past years has given substantially to our organization and for a variety of reasons has become somewhat inactive. In speaking with him, today, he reported to me about a meeting that had occurred in India of international dimensions and he went into a fair amount of detail about the meeting, describing exactly the meeting that your wife was in. And I informed him that your wife was there as a keynote speaker. It shocked him to hear that, it was a good confirmation of the work that you have already done.

So the question then, since you and Helga and the organization at large, but specifically you and Helga, have tipped it over in Russia, in China, in India, and other nations that have joined this new paradigm already. In the United States we really have just a small tipping to do, actually, and I appreciate your using that "tip," so that we can be more optimistic that we can simply "tip" it in and get the job done, but that has to still be done. Is there any comment that you have for us to get that small, yet necessary, action required to fight for that last inch?

It's Working Now

LaRouche: Well it's not that tough. It is tough, but it's not that tough. I've been at this for a long time, you know, and so we often get a near access to reshaping the policies of history. And if we get a chance once in a while, we are capable of doing that. I have done a good deal of that in my life—I guess 60 years or so since I've been doing this kind of thing. So I'm familiar with this.

And what we do, what I do, and what Helga does now, is to bring into play the understanding of the issue to be considered, which will lead to a solution. In other words, you've got people out there,— they're talking about this, they're talking about that, they're concerned about this, they're concerned about that. The problem is, how can you bring the people involved—correctly—

painted by Charles R. Leslie (1793-1879)

Henry C. Carey (above), a strong backer of the American System, fought to eradicate the British Empire system. LaRouche noted that there is a powerful force, represented by Russia and China, which could "create a new form of development for mankind" to defeat that system.

not by a swindle or anything like that, but just correctly to come to a decision to say, "wait a minute, this is the key, this is good? This is the key." And when people see the point is the key and they don't give up on that, then they're able to operate. For example, what's happened with Russia? The history of Russia in modern times, and particularly in the recent period—the change that occurred in terms of the recent operation by Putin. Or, what's happening with China? China, the key. Putin, the key! These are the leading forces throughout the planet. Putin and China. Now India. These are the leading edges, of forces of change for a better world.

We are about to do a job on the study of China, with the idea of the development of the back of the Moon. What is the secret behind the back of the Moon? Now, the back of the Moon is not just some fantasy. The back of the Moon is a very specific kind of physical principle. That principle, when properly understood, will change the history of mankind.

In the space program that was developed earlier, the original space program, this thing had the same purpose. What we did recently, with our program in Texas, same thing: That's what works. Now you have to keep working at it. You don't get a free ride, unless you're very, very lucky. But if you get the right idea, get the key, you can discover the principle which will make it work. But it takes work.

Question: I was looking at some of Henry C. Carey's work *The Harmony of Interests,* and one of the things I noticed was his clear commitment in trying to eliminate the British Empire's ideology, or whatever you want to call it, but I see his sense of eradicating it in himself and also showing that power to others, to eliminate this empire. I wanted to see if you can show that through this energy that resides in man, we can actually eliminate this threat.

LaRouche: There's no doubt about that. The problem we face now, on that account, in a practical form of expression, is limited to certain parts of the planet. For example, you will find that Russia is now in a mode of form in its work which is on the road to victory. It has not reached victory, but it's on the road to victory. There are revolutions in terms of economy in that region that are influenced by those who are associated as allies of the same forces as Putin.

China: The power of China is immense! China was naturally a very powerful nation, intrinsically. But it had to turn that intrinsic power into an actual effect. Now, under the new administration they have done that. What has happened now? We find a movement in Asia, in the Asian region in particular, which is really moving!

The British? Ha! To be a Briton? That is the worst thing that can happen to you! I mean, they are the most unfortunate people on the planet, the British officials and so forth. My Scottish ancestors are still aching about what happened, back in that century.

So, therefore, we are in a situation where there is a great force, a powerful force which is able to be mobilized and is being mobilized which can create a new form of development for mankind. This is one which will be based largely on the far side of the Moon. Why? Well, people have never understood what the Moon really represented. People know about the Moon. They take some measurements, they've done some investigations. But they still haven't solved what the Moon really means. Now, if the project which is available and in process, is put into effect, we will now find out what the meaning of the Moon is.

Now, as to what the meaning of the Moon is, you will say, "well, don't we know all about the Moon?" Well, you don't know all about the Moon. You don't know what the back side of the Moon is, or what it looks like. You don't know what the factors are. And what is happening now, is China is going into that area, to work on the back side of the Moon and find out how this thing works. This is something that was done by a great scientist in the postwar period in the same way.

So we're now back to work. We're getting rid of Obama, throwing him out to someplace where we won't notice him. And that is going to give us the means to get a better understanding. Remember—we had a space program. We had a space program. The space program was very efficient. It was scientifically correct. It was not refined to the extent we might wish, but it was perfect as an operation. Now, we're going back to that.

We now are kicking Obama out of the system, get him out of there, and we're going back to see—well, China's doing this, on the back side of the Moon—now

we're going to get a real insight into what is going on in the Solar System. And we're going to get that soon if we continue the project. We will begin to get revelations on the future of mankind in the Solar system. We will get that. And the work of China right now, on the far side of the Moon work, will help us very much. There are things in Russia which have similar correlations, less significant but very important.

The development of China, the rate of development of the population of China under these recent conditions, this is a spectacular big leap! Don't underestimate it in any way! And then, there are Russia, China and other countries which are now grouping together. They're moving to move for mankind! Get rid of these evil things! Move for mankind! And don't change the subject.

Manhattan Has a Potential

Question: [from the Internet] Lyn, we've got a question from someone on the Internet. He's a West Coast gentlemen of originally Persian extraction. He says that the Saudis and Turkey keep assembling hundreds of troops on the Syrian border. Do you think there is a danger that they might actually invade?

LaRouche: Absolutely. No question about that. The question is, will they be permitted to invade? And that means two things: It means the way in which the problem is attacked, and the thing is what the solution might be to win the fight. And I think we have some pretty possibilities of victory in that respect. I don't think we have a completed victory, but we do have the option, and we should stick together in this area, with Putin's participation and with what is coming from inside Russia, what is going on in India, what is going on in China. These factors are very important factors. And as they are coordinated, they are very powerful factors. Just have to work at it.

Question: I would like to give a report on the progress of fundraising. Since the children are enrolled in this movement, it has made a big impact on the families. Such as our children are teaching the parents about the future, instead of the reverse, which is really good.

I'm confident this will be extraordinary in the coming weeks. And this will continue. What is your advice?

LaRouche: Let's take the area of Manhattan, right? Manhattan is a very important center in the United States, extremely important. Now, not everybody is good. We have a lot of drunks, of course, in Manhattan from time to time, and things like that. But we do find that Manhattan does have a potential of providing people who are committed to doing things which are useful and good. And one of the major things we should look for, in what we're doing,— because we know, that is, we understand Manhattan. Despite everything else that's different than that, everything else that stinks, everything that's wrong, there is in Manhattan a concentration of people, of institutions and people, who actually have qualifications to do something.

For example, take that Wall Street area, take the whole Manhattan area—the big block of giant structures? And you look at it and you say, "is this something we want? Is this something, an El Cheapo kind of thing that we have to be ashamed of, or that sort of thing?" No, you say, "well, why don't we just twist this thing a little bit, so that we get the right things to come into place, as opposed to the wrong things?" And I have quite an experience with Manhattan, various kinds of experiences. And all you have to do, is get the right twist from the option, and get the people involved in this, and you will find that everything will change, not completely, but it will become an overwhelming change. And that's about the best shot that you can get in these situations.

If you can become the overriding influence over the development of an area like Manhattan, around it, if you can do that, you can change the whole thing around, because the others will have to give way. I spent a good deal of time in Manhattan, and I can tell you, I've seen that effect many times. For example, there's a building up there on the street where I used to live, in the museum [American Museum of Natural History], the animal museum,— all kinds of things. And it's a beautiful place, it actually is, from the standpoint of function. Now, all you have to do is go in there, and you can look at the thing and say, "this is a piece of junk." Or, somebody else looks at it, and says, "Hey! We're learning something about the future of humanity, from periods prior to the emergence of mankind. And this is something we have to cite." Once you get that view from that standpoint, you're on the road to victory, if you stick at it.

It's Happening in Texas

Question: I've been following the Presidential election, and the way I'm looking at it is, you've got two candidates who are totally unthinkable: I mean you've got the Killer Hillary Clinton, and this Apeman Donald Trump, who is really the lowest of the low. Those people are just unthinkable. And then you've got this guy Bernie Sanders, who nobody gives much of a chance to. And I'm not saying he's anything special— not at all! Or that the programs he's recommending, they're kind of wishy-washy and everything, but I'd say he, as opposed to the other two, he is a human being, is somebody you could think of as being a President, and somebody who would listen to—and whose supporters will listen to—our progressive ideas about the New Silk Road and the space program and all that. That is our natural audience, I think.

So what I think is, we're coming down to the actual election, eight months away. I don't think Obama is going to be impeached or removed between now and the election, and I think we have to look forward, you know. Not just live in the present, and say "we have to impeach him now," but look forward and say, "well, we've probably got to put up with him for another eight months," and so let's get prepared for the next President, and let's see if we can make it somebody who's at least thinkable and we can possibly work with.

So, I say, let's destroy Hillary Clinton, destroy Donald Trump, destroy 'em, nuke 'em, whatever it takes, and then, Sanders is sort of reasonably milquetoast but at least human, would be the last man standing and we could work with him for the next eight years! That's the way I'm looking at it.

LaRouche: That won't work. That absolutely— that policy will not work! It cannot work. It will be disaster. You have to dump the whole thing, the whole problem. Dump it over. There's nothing good waiting for you from the election process now.

Yes, it looks like now Hillary's got a position. So-and-so's got a position, so-and-so's got a position. That's so-called. Forget it! Because if you want to bet on that thing, you're going to lose! If you support that cause, you're going to lose! You're going to be finished!

So therefore, despite everything that people try to tell you, don't believe any of it—But rather, look at the thing more carefully, and there is no one who is a compromise candidate, who's going to save anything for you.

Question: [from the Internet] I have a question related to the breakdown crisis in the trans-Atlantic, that comes from a supporter in San Juan, Puerto Rico. He asked the following:

"My question is, What can the ordinary citizens do to save themselves and others in the midst of this economic crisis, when our leaders say there are no short-term solutions and we do not seem to have any new leaders stepping up with solutions to replace the ones who say they don't have solutions?"

LaRouche: Okay, I can make a very explicit portrait of what this means. First of all, all of these things, usual discussion things, forget it, they're fake, they don't mean a thing. Because what's happened is, as long as the United States and the members of the United States organization believe in this kind of thing, this kind of policy that the present electoral process would suggest,— is junk! You will get nothing but bad news and a bad future from that, if you stick to that. You have to think about how do you dump these guys?

Now, what I do know is what is in process, throughout the parts of the leading circles in the United States— I'm talking about people who are leading in economic and related kinds of things, but who are intelligent people, and they are very much disturbed by their awareness that this system as it's working now, cannot, in any way succeed. In other words, no matter what you think you're going to get, you're going to get something bad. You have to change the policy.

But the smart people, and there are smart people out there, who do understand something about how the economy works, they do have an appreciation about what is true and what is false,— they are troubled. They have been habituated to trying to adapt to a condition which they know can't work. Then you are looking for those people to start thinking about what can work. And that process is happening it's happening in places in Texas. They know that this thing has to change. They know that all this stuff, the electoral rallies and so forth are just junk. They don't mean anything. They couldn't possibly succeed.

So there is no future which can be based on a continuation of current trends. You have to get rid of the current trends, and pretty much fast.

That's what we're doing now. We're going back to the space program. We're going back into Texas, where the space program was based, the concentration. Obama came along and Obama shut down the space program. The space program was shut. We have reopened the basis of the space program. We're working on it! And there are people who are looking at it with open eyes, saying, "Hey, wait a minute, this will work. It has to work, nothing else will work." And that's the way you have to look at it.

Don't think you can get a cheap solution. You can

get your neck cut off, more likely. So you have to earn an achievement of a method of action, which will actually bring benefits to mankind. And you have to find those opportunities, you have to concentrate on them, grip them and use them, and base the future of mankind on the goods.

The Alternative to War

Question: You recently made a statement about having two choices or making two decisions: one is to live, and the other is to die. Well, obviously, what China and the Silk Road represent is the decision to live, where the British system and Obama's intent to continue to provoke and start World War III is obviously the decision to die. In that context, could you share your thoughts with the current state of North Korea, please?

LaRouche: The North Korea thing is not as bad as it looks. It's bad because of the fact that it is in a bad situation. But there's no reason why there couldn't be a rational solution for the crisis so-called, of North Korea. And the sooner that people in that region recognize that fact and act on that fact, the quicker we'll get out of the whole mess.

For example, you know, you're looking in this area, North Korea. And you have on the one side, you have China, and as China, the railway route. And the railway route from that part comes into North Korea. Then you come to the other line from North Korea and it goes into an area which is aimed at Russia. If you put these connections together, and you look at all these considerations, you say, "well, what we've got here is a railroad map. And if we put this railroad map to work, and function, we ought to be able to bring some peace among these people, to avoid foolish nonsense." And, at the same time, you can mobilize the people to bring into action the three-part railway system—one a railway system which comes in from China, the next step is one that comes to North Korea. The next step is the one that runs into Russia—well, why not just open the whole thing up? Come to an agreement, a common agreement, and develop the whole territory. Then everybody's satisfied.

And therefore, what you have to do in a case like this, you have a bunch of people running around screaming at the top of their heads, and under the bottom of their ass or something, but get them off that stuff! You have to give them a sense that they have a future! They have a future! And the future has keys to it: those keys will bring the richness of life for people in that area.

Just think, take the route from China into North

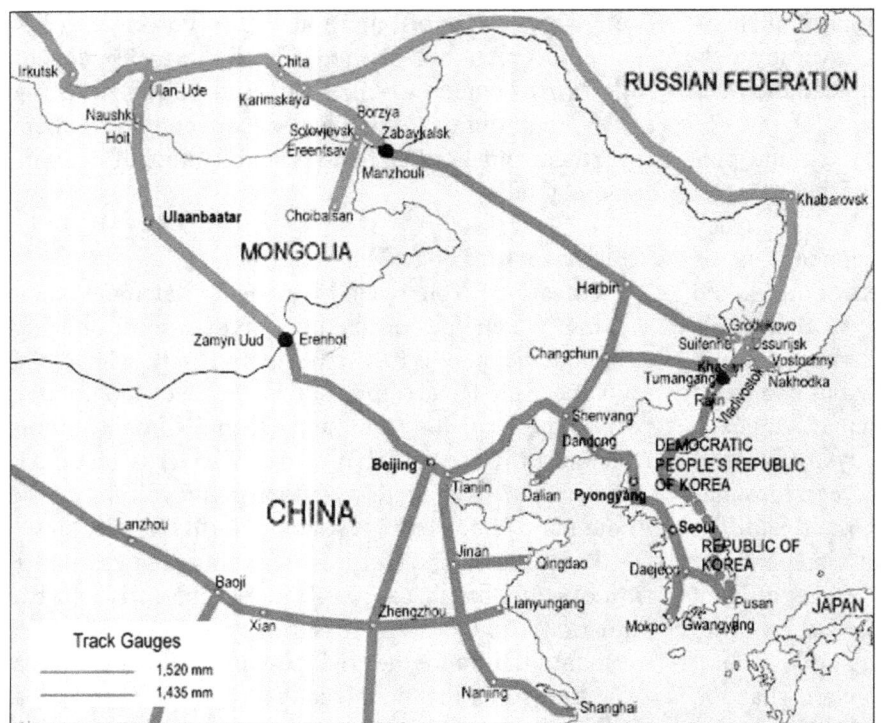

The Asia-wide railroad grid being developed by China, which can end the isolation of North Korea, provides an alternative to war.

Korea, from North Korea into Russia. It's a simple route. It's been sitting there for a long time, since World War II. All you have to do, is make an agreement based on that idea.

So, therefore, what you have to do is propose competent solutions which will give you the alternatives to avoid war.

Mankind Has a Destiny

Question: [from the Internet] Why do you go back to the idea of Nicholas of Cusa and *imago viva Dei?* Is that still something we need we need to refer to, is that still the core nature of real religious belief?

LaRouche: That becomes difficult because in point of fact, those examples which are backed from history, the specific ones you mention, these are valid. They are not a completion of a solution for a design. But they indicate the kind of behavior which human beings will follow, if they wish to make progress, in terms of human progress.

So it's not a map, it's not someone with a formula. What there is, is the development,— the history of Brunelleschi, for example. Brunelleschi's a good example of this kind of thing. Here he was, he was a goldsmith, he was the greatest genius of his lifetime. He was the most effective person in terms of development of science at that time. There were earlier periods of scientific progress, but Brunelleschi was the real miracle. He did all kinds of things, great improvisation, creations which were unknown to people of his own time, all these kinds of things.

And so therefore, there is a course in the development of mankind, which goes way back through history, where mankind progresses, and the fact that mankind can progress and should progress is something which should be steered. But you always have to have a light before you. You have to see the future, beyond. And that's the way this thing works: You have to see the future beyond. And you see what might be the case, you think what might be the solution, and you find out something that you see is possibly the solution, and then you apply that approximate solution to the future.

That's the best thing that mankind has done, in practical terms in general, and Brunelleschi, in that particular period, is one of the most important parts of history for mankind during that time.

Question: [from the Internet] There was a report about the return of an American astronaut coming back on a Russian vehicle from the International Space Station. This fellow Scott Kelley just came back to Earth recently. Apparently, the report is that this astronaut came back—when he landed he was two inches taller than when he left, apparently, according to the individual writing this note.

So a report of the U.S.-Russia cooperation is quite exciting, and one of our supporters asks from San Francisco, "what can we do now to ensure that the United States keeps doing exciting things like this" work in space?

LaRouche: I don't know that we can get everybody becoming taller by this method. But I would say that the fact that this happened, or could happen, is quite relevant. See, mankind is not an animal, contrary to Obama, for example, or something like that.

The point is that mankind is intended and designed to develop its own powers, in ways which enable mankind to realize and captivate the ability to create new states in human nature, absolutely new conditions, conditions that have never been known by any species before. And that's what mankind has been able to do.

Now therefore, we say, this leads to another question: Because we say, how does this work? Well, what works is the fact that mankind is a creative force, intrinsically. The human species is a creative force. And the creative force undergoes development. For example, every child could express, and desire to express, the assumption that every human being born after the child had the opportunity of becoming superior in knowledge and efficiency for the future of mankind. In other words the whole purpose of this thing is not how to get mankind to be more successful and so forth. What you're trying to do is get the human species to develop to a higher level of development, of capabilities, and that's what you're looking for. In the school systems today is a bunch of idiocy. It's rotten and idiocy! Because the child, the importance of the human species,— the child should be able to reach powers of development which the parents and grandparents had never been able to reach! So therefore, the point of the whole thing is that mankind is developing into the universe. That the universe is being changed by mankind's development. And the promotion of that kind of progress is the most essential thing about mankind.

When you say, you'll try to fix mankind: this is who you are, this is your limit. You can't go any further. You want to be a monkey? We'll make you a monkey.

But the truth of the matter is that mankind is able to progress, because mankind, we know, we can prove that mankind is capable, voluntarily, of achieving things in space which mankind could not otherwise achieve.

And it's that fact: mankind has a destiny in the stars. Mankind has a destiny in the future of space and time. And mankind must develop as such, in order to achieve those kinds of higher achievements. And that's what the

FILIPPO BRVNELLESCHI SCVL.E. ARCHIT.
FIORENTINO

Mankind must see the future, beyond, said LaRouche, to achieve its destiny, and stated that by so doing, Brunelleschi was "the most effective person in terms of development of science at that time."

issue is. The species must be improved. The species must be self-improved. We must turn babies into geniuses.

Question: [from the Internet] In the recent couple of weeks, as you know, organizers have been going to various public meetings, challenging speakers on the failure of U.S. foreign policy. Apparently we went to two events today at Stanford University, and the report is that even some really kind of rotten people, who are well-known figures, are now getting slightly freaked out because nothing seems to be working.

Do you have a comment on this? Because it appears, as everything is falling apart, that even some people who are somewhat disgusting, are now becoming slightly unnerved, which seems to indicate that we're at the edge of some very, very big potential change. Do you have any comment?

LaRouche: I would say it's like the idea of spanking the child. Sometimes history spanks the children because they realize that all the little nasty things they wanted to do, don't work! And what they try to do with that gets worse and worse and worse and worse! And they want to say, "What do I do to get free of this pain?!" And that's the way you do it. And that's what's happening.

There are people inside the United States, significant people, and also internationally, who realize that all the things that they think would work, were a flop, a big failure, a disaster. And they say, "Please, tell me what the solution is?" And that's what they're asking for. And you have to get sympathy for them, to say, "What is it, in you, that will enable you to be free of a perpetual disaster built into you, currently?" You feel good, then.

Question: I just want to thank Lyn and Helga LaRouche for taking the High Silk Road. That is my comment for the night. We are just so grateful for your taking the high road, and showing people that they can be creative and productive. That does make a difference for the well being of everybody. Thank you.

LaRouche: Thank you!

A CONTRIBUTION TO AN ONGOING DISCUSSION

For an Economic Recovery: Think Like MacArthur!

by Robert Ingraham

And what we have to understand, we have to go back and say, "we once had a great United States. It was led by Alexander Hamilton." He was the great genius who made the creation of the United States possible. There were many other people who participated, but it was a teamwork which centered around him, Hamilton. Which typifies what makes a nation work, which makes a nation successful.

And therefore, we have to focus, not on this thing, or that thing, or this thing; you have to think about, how do you bring the forces of an entire nation, and among nations, into a kind of cooperation which more or less smoothly moves people upward, in terms of their own morals, and their intellectual levels and so forth. That's what the issue is.

After you get that thing, now you can sit back and say, "well, what are we talking about?" and let the people who are interested sit down and tell each other, what they were talking about.
—Lyndon LaRouche,
National Fireside Chat, Feb. 25, 2016

March 3—The present economic, social, and moral crisis confronting both the United States and Western Europe is deadly. It is all-encompassing. So far, virtually all proposals and initiatives which have emanated from elected U.S. leaders on how to deal with this crisis have been pathetic and represent a failure of both thinking and judgment. Many Americans have made piecemeal or pragmatic proposals to deal with various aspects of this crisis. Oftentimes, this takes the form of pointing to specific initiatives from the past as solutions to today's problems. None of this will work. There is only one path out of this crisis, and it will require a dramatic strategic reorientation of the United States and a determination to break the power of the British Empire permanently. What is required is not a "financial reform" approach but rather, a fundamental change in both U.S. strategy and the thinking of the American people.

This offering will hopefully shed light on this necessary approach, this necessary quality of thinking which is required if we are to overcome the onrushing economic breakdown crisis and concurrent escalation toward world war—if we are to act in time to save both the people of our nation and the rest of the world. To provide for our beleaguered citizens hope, opportunity, and a better future.

To clarify: Many people view the worsening crisis in the trans-Atlantic region as one of a financial/monetary bankruptcy. This view has the tail wagging the dog. The crisis is fundamentally and foremost one of a profound decline and breakdown of the physical productive capabilities of Europe and the Americas, and the effect that breakdown has had on the minds and morality of the population. It is not a domestic American crisis; it is a strategic crisis. That grasp of the true nature of the problem is why, in this report, we will leave the question of U.S. monetary reform to the end. It is the least important and the easiest to solve.

A second distinguishing aspect to this report involves the insight that no recipe, no fixed program for economic recovery, can possibly work. Nor will any attempt to simply resurrect specific measures from the past be successful. As Lyndon LaRouche has emphasized, the first critical action which must be taken is to shut down Wall Street. This means wiping out the values of the quadrillions of dollars of speculative debt which now exist, without compensation, and shutting down the institutions which engage in such gambling activity. While certain past weapons in defense of the nation which have proven their devastating effectiveness—such as Franklin Roosevelt's Glass-Steagall legislation—are needed today to exterminate the cancer known as Wall Street, upon more serious reflection, it should be understood that the most urgent necessity is not to be found in the specifics of this or that program, but in a recognition that since the death of Franklin Roosevelt, the United States has increasingly become

In the Korean War, despite violent opposition and outright sabotage, Gen. Douglas MacArthur executed a surprise landing behind enemy lines at Inchon, which led to the rout of the North Korean army. Here, MacArthur (seated) observes the shelling of Inchon from the U.S.S. Mount McKinley on the day of the landing, Sept. 15, 1950.

U.S. National Archives

subservient to and integrated with the practices of the British Empire.

Our current President is a British puppet, and Wall Street is nothing but an extension of the British imperial financial system. Our current culture is entirely a trans-Atlantic culture, a culture defined by the practices, immorality, and outlook of the British Empire. A culture which is dying, which is murdering itself. The only path to an American economic recovery is to end the current trans-Atlantic relationship and to wipe out all vestiges of the British Empire, including such disgusting British marcher-lords as the Kingdom of Saudi Arabia and the Muslim Brotherhood government of Turkey.

The three American Presidents who accomplished the greatest advances in the productive economic development of the nation were George Washington, Abraham Lincoln, and Franklin Roosevelt. Washington, with the benefit of Alexander Hamilton's genius, created our system of political economy and national public credit. Lincoln, under wartime conditions, did things which Hamilton had never attempted. Roosevelt crushed his Wall Street opponents and uplifted the condition of the entire nation through a series of revolutionary measures. What was common to all of them was a guiding principle of future-orientation, the advancement of productivity and creative human potential, combined with a fierce opposition to the outlook and practices of the British Empire.

Although his Presidency was aborted by the bullet of a British assassin, John Kennedy also demonstrated the same qualities in his Rice University speech and his creation of the Apollo space mission. These men were all different. They did not copy programmatic recipes from the past; they invented, they created, they adopted new approaches to achieve results that were coherent with their underlying intent and principles. Such is the outlook that is needed today.

I. Taking the Military Approach

On March 3, 1864 Lincoln promoted Ulysses Grant to Lieutenant General, giving him command of all Union Armies. At that time, despite the Union victories at Gettysburg and Vicksburg, most of the Southern territory was still under Confederate control. Union military operations were stalled, and treasonous efforts were well-advanced in the North to remove Lincoln as President in the upcoming November elections.

In the Summer of 1950, Douglas MacArthur was placed in command of all United Nations forces in Korea. The military situation was desperate. South Korean and United Nations forces had been driven back

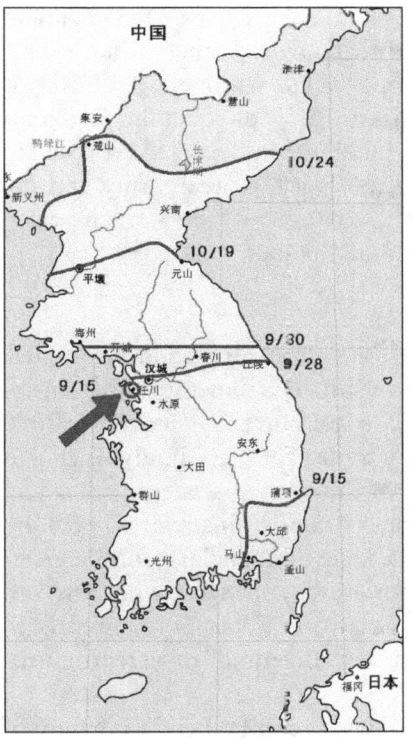

The Inchon landing in 1950 and its dramatic aftermath. The boundary in the southeast corner labeled 9/15 (the Pusan Pocket) shows the position of MacArthur's troops on Sept. 15. The large arrow shows the Inchon landing that day. The boundary near the top, labeled 10/24, shows the position of troops on Oct. 24, just five weeks later.

to a small region, the Pusan Pocket, in the southeastern corner of the Korean peninsula. The North Korean army was a hair's breadth away from total victory.

In the case of Grant, in the Spring of 1864, in consultation with Abraham Lincoln and William Sherman, he devised a war-winning strategy and deployed his forces for victory. On May 4, 1864 Grant's army crossed the Rapidan River in Virginia, moving into the Wilderness, thus initiating the Overland Campaign that would end in the capture of Richmond and the surrender of Robert E. Lee. Three days later, on May 7, 1864, Sherman's army left Chattanooga, Tennessee, heading toward Atlanta. Eleven months later the war was won.

In July of 1950, facing almost certain defeat in Korea, Douglas MacArthur put forward his plan for a surprise amphibious landing behind enemy lines. Due to violent opposition and outright sabotage by other military commanders, as well as top officials within the Truman Administration, the plan was delayed,— but the final realization of the Inchon Landing, on Sept. 15, 1950, led to the complete rout of the North Korean army and the occupation of almost the entirety of the Korean peninsula by UN forces in mid-October.

Library of Congress

Gen. Ulysses S. Grant at his Cold Harbor, Va., headquarters. In the spring of 1864, in consultation with President Lincoln and Gen. William Tecumseh Sherman, he devised a war-winning strategy. Eleven months after deployment, the war was won.

Wartime Operations

The lesson to be learned from Grant and MacArthur is one of strategic leadership. It is imperative that Americans recognize that we are currently under war-time conditions, and thus, we must act accordingly. Trying to deal with the reality of the current strategic crisis and meltdown of the trans-Atlantic financial system by simply proposing a package of financial reform legislation, or proposing a series of recipes that will "solve all the problems," will not work. What is required is to think, so to speak, "through the mind" of a creative military commander.

The first prerequisite is to comprehend the nature of the battlefield on which you are fighting. What defines the essence of the war? What constitutes victory, i.e., winning the peace? The choosing of allies, based upon agreement on commonly shared principles, is also essential. Lastly, success is not possible without a determined, single-minded commitment to victory.

No wars, whether military, economic, or cultural, are ever identical to those of the past. To succeed today it is essential to recognize what is different, what has changed, from the challenges confronted by Washington, Hamilton, Lincoln, and Roosevelt. We are not fighting the battles of 1789, 1861, or 1933. We must fully appreciate the precise nature of the battlefield in 2016.

The most profound change from those earlier times, a change whose implications are still greatly underappreciated, is that America is no longer alone. In the time of Washington, Lincoln, and the Roosevelt of 1933, the United States existed in a world economic and financial environment controlled by the British empire. London-centered economic and strategic attacks against the United States were incessant. In those past times there did not exist any global combination of forces able to overthrow London's world hegemony.

This is no longer true. The economic power, and the new economic directionality, already exhibited in the BRICS, the Shanghai Cooperation Organization, and China's One Belt, One Road policy have already transformed and is continuing to transform the potentials for mankind's development. Strategically, the great economic might wielded by the nations working with Russia and China already dwarfs that of the trans-Atlantic community. Simply put, America does not need to create from scratch a new world economic dynamic; we simply need to join one that is already in existence. If the United States allies with Russia, China, and India the power will exist to end the British Empire. London's power can be broken suddenly, irrevocably—and *now!*

Hsin Chong Construction Group

The new economic directionality exhibited in the BRICS, the Shanghai Cooperation Organization, and China's One Belt, One Road policy is transforming the potentials for mankind's development. Shown here is La Viva, a part of Tieling New Town, one of many completely new cities recently built in China. China projects outward its impulse to build for humanity by means of the One Belt, One Road policy and the related institutions.

The policies and practices of the British Empire can be eradicated from the Earth.

A second, equally critical change in the battlefield is to recognize that the America of today is not the America of 1789, 1861, or 1933. Since the death of Franklin Roosevelt, the United States, step-by-step, has merged its identity and its policies with those of the trans-Atlantic system, i.e., the outlook and culture of the British Empire. The enemies of America have repealed or nullified the policies and philosophy of the Roosevelt Administration. The United States today has joined and is allied with precisely those very forces which must be crushed.

Therefore, in the mind of a military commander, considering the nature of the present battlefield, the following conditions need to be taken into account:

1) A war-winning coalition of forces, a coalition which can agree to a basic set of principles, already exists.

2) America must replace its allegiance to the British-controlled trans-Atlantic system and re-orient to Asia. This can only be done by removing Obama from the Presidency and shutting down Wall Street.

3) It is urgent that the United States return to the economic outlook of Alexander Hamilton. Nothing can be accomplished without taking that step. In accordance with this approach, all aspects of new proposed U.S. policy must reflect those sentiments expressed in the First Inaugural, and the First and Second Fireside Chats—all by Franklin Roosevelt.

4) A combination of leading persons within the United States, i.e., the equivalent of a military General Staff, must come together to effect a radical shift in U.S. strategic thinking. America's economic and strategic future is in Asia.

5) Pre-emptive actions must be taken now; such actions can not wait until 2017. The escalating danger of all-out global military conflict must be pre-empted by a change in U.S. policy.

There can be no compromise on this approach, no compromise on the full annihilation of the British Empire. Total victory is achievable. What will undermine and destroy that potential for victory is political prostitution, such as settling for superficial "practical" reforms. What will ensure defeat is acquiescence to the power of London and Wall Street.

II. Saving the People and Creating the Future

The social and economic situation within the United States is horrific. Most of the nation's industrial base is gone. Infrastructure is rotting away. Almost 100 million Americans are now classified as "not in the labor force," which is simply an Orwellian euphemism for saying that they are unemployed. Skill levels have collapsed. Millions are homeless. Tens of millions of youth are uneducated and unskilled. Drug consumption and deaths by overdose are epidemic.

Where To Start and What To Prioritize?

The first requirement, as in Roosevelt's case and as in Lincoln's case, is to demonstrate to the people of the nation an unshakable moral commitment to their future. The leaders of the nation must make clear, as Roosevelt did, that the President and the elected representatives of the people will act on behalf of the people and for the future of the nation. This must be done, and it must be honest. The pessimism, the cynicism, the hopelessness must end.

A plan of attack must be formulated, and it must pursue several different goals simultaneously. The attack must start at once and it must be aggressively pursued. Prior to any action, however, a change in thinking must occur. It will be necessary to adopt a standard upon which all economic decisions will be based. That standard, as it was for Alexander Hamilton, is a recognition of the fundamental distinction between human beings and beasts. All economic, as well as other "social" policy must be intended to revive and promote a truly human outlook within the population. All policy initiatives should be aimed at promoting and enhancing the creative potentials within the population. An economic recovery is not about "making more money;" it is about advancing the condi-

Public domain

First, rescue Americans facing poverty, hopelessness, even death. Here, Camden, N.J., in 2009, one of the poorest U.S. cities.

tion of our species within the Universe and enhancing those creative abilities which make us truly human.

The immediate necessary economic initiatives will fall generally into three categories.

First, the government must act, and act forcefully, to rescue those Americans now facing poverty, hopelessness, even death. The most vulnerable—children, the elderly, the sick, veterans, the abject poor—must be defended for the duration of the crisis. This will require direct immediate government action, including food, housing, adequate pensions, and medical care. Whatever needs to be spent must be spent. This will require a

---

Happiness Lies in the Thrill of Creative Effort

Happiness lies not in the mere possession of money; it lies in the joy of achievement, in the thrill of creative effort. The joy and moral stimulation of work no longer must be forgotten in the mad chase of evanescent profits. These dark days will be worth all they cost us if they teach us that our true destiny is not to be ministered unto but to minister to ourselves and to our fellow men.

Recognition of the falsity of material wealth as the standard of success goes hand in hand with the abandonment of the false belief that public office and high political position are to be valued only by the standards of pride of place and personal profit; and there must be an end to a conduct in banking and in business which too often has given to a sacred trust the likeness of callous and selfish wrongdoing. Small wonder that confidence languishes, for it thrives only on honesty, on honor, on the sacredness of obligations, on faithful protection, on unselfish performance; without them it cannot live.

—from Franklin Roosevelt's First Inaugural Address

中国航天科技集团公司
China Aerospace Science and Technology Corporation

Xinhua

Second, we must act on the future. The wondrous Chinese space initiatives, together with those of Russia, India, and many other nations, are moving rapidly forward. All we have to do is join them in friendship and cooperation. Here, a model of China's Mars probe, planned to land on Mars in 2021.

Harry Hopkins-style, hands-on day-to-day commitment. Over time, under conditions of sustained economic recovery, many of these conditions will be ameliorated, but for now, no government that honors the profound personal morality of Abraham Lincoln can tolerate throwing tens of millions of fellow Americans on the scrap heap.

Second, we must act on the future. We are not simply trying to recover what has been lost. Revolutionary challenges and vision are what will move us into the future. There is a term called a "Science Driver," but that term is often used banally to simply reflect such things as spin-off technologies from scientific research. It actually signifies something more profound. Today, LaRouche PAC leader Kesha Rogers has called for an immediate return to the full Kennedy-era agenda for the space program. That is a Science Driver. Nothing else comes close to striking at the heart of the human potential, to unleashing both an infusion of national cultural optimism as well as the necessary challenges in science and frontier human investigation. This represents mankind's future, while at the same time it defines for the entire population what the nature of a true human identity is.

The wondrous Chinese space initiatives, together with those of Russia, India, and many other nations, are moving rapidly forward. All we have to do is join with them in friendship and cooperation. That's all

there is to it. Simply, make the decision to join with these other nations in this effort. They are waiting for us—with open arms—to do just that. Given America's space expertise and experience, if we collaborate with China and her friends, the results will quickly surpass anything that was accomplished in the 1960s. The exploration of our Solar system and the Galaxy beyond will define the new human identity.

What we do in space and what we discover there will pose new revolutionary questions and problems for the human species. For example, nothing will be successful unless the nations of the world recognize the discovery of the principle of the back side of the Moon. When we find out what is behind the Moon, which is being worked on by the Chinese, new insights and never-before recognized principles which govern our Solar system and our Galaxy will begin to emerge. These will then define a new set of challenges.

It is this orientation, a future orientation, which has been snuffed out by U.S. subservience to the British Empire.

The **third** area of economic action which will be required is to rebuild the physical economic potential of the nation. This will require a broad review of manufacturing, agriculture, transportation, infrastructure, education, health care, and other key areas. The government must act to prevent any further erosion in these areas, and begin a process, involving the national government, state governments, and the private sector, to begin to develop new capabilities coherent with national goals, e.g., high-speed rail, nuclear power, and water desalinization. This will take time, but it must be started at once. China's example, in this regard, is noteworthy.

There is also the question of national youth unemployment, now over 50%. Again, one can not simply copy the example of the Civilian Conservation Corps, and it should not be the intention to channel unemployed youth into primarily unskilled labor. Rather, new educational methods will be needed, not simply for "job-training," but for improving the cognition, the skills, and the potentials of young Americans. We have to re-awaken in the minds and souls of our young people

Third, we must rebuild the physical economic potential of the nation, applying the American System of Alexander Hamilton. Is China's President Xi more American than today's Americans? Here, Xi with his old American friends in Muscatine, Iowa. In 1985 he was part of a Chinese delegation studying American agriculture, and stayed with an American family in Muscatine.

the desire to make discoveries. As national goals for rebuilding cities and infrastructure are defined, together with opportunities in even more advanced scientific work, millions of youth will be provided with the chance for a productive future.

Allies in War

If America had to do all of this on her own, the potential for ultimate success were dubious. But we don't. The world is currently gripped by a deadly strategic confrontation, as the British Empire desperately attempts to preserve its existence. If the United States joins with Russia and China, that Empire can be eradicated. Then many things become possible.

The question of economic recovery or economic policy for the United States is not a domestic issue. This is a strategic battle. Lyndon LaRouche located this reality in the following way during his Feb. 27, 2016 Dialogue with the Manhattan Project:

On the other hand you have the Russian mode and the Chinese mode and other things related to the same which are on the upscale. So, obviously, there's not a complementarity of voices,

but rather a conflict, a very significant conflict. Do you want to live or die? That's the difference. If you want to follow Obama, if you want to work with the British royal family, then you're doomed. If you want to get a succession for a new world system and you're able to do it, together with Russia, China, India and so forth, this is a different voice. The one voice, the old voice, is the evil voice. It's the evil voice of stupidity and corruption. That's the voice of Obama and the British.

On the other hand what Putin represents and what China represents, right now, and now India coming in, in a very significant way, in a resurrection kind of way, and these things are going to develop.

The trans-Atlantic alliance, which was created at the moment that Franklin Roosevelt was placed in his grave, has been an horrendous historic failure. It represents the greatest crime against the American Republic since its founding. That British Empire/trans-Atlantic system is now doomed. If, at this historic moment, America remains locked into the trans-Atlantic world and fails to adopt a Pacific orientation, then the people of the United States are doomed. No legislation, no "program," no "reform" will change that.

We must make a shift toward Asia. Under conditions of an alliance with China, India, and Putin's Russia, an economic recovery becomes possible. Look at the projects being planned or built by the BRICS and the SCO. Look at the projects proposed in the North American extension of the Eurasian Land-Bridge, including the proposed Bering Strait connection. We must join that process. Abandon the dying trans-Atlantic system and join with Asia. New industries, infrastructure, and a shutting down of narcotics trafficking then become possible. But nothing will work without the strategic reorientation. Nothing will work until the power of the British Empire is destroyed.

26 Far Side of the Moon

EIR March 11, 2016

III. Dealing with Money

The trans-Atlantic London/Wall Street financial system, a system of unbridled financial gambling, is dead, merely awaiting the faint breeze which will topple it. However, it will not go quietly, and it will not surrender. Pre-emptive action is urgently required now.

This is not an academic discussion. The entire financial house of cards could blow apart at any moment, with financial defaults ranging into the hundreds of trillions of dollars, generating a tsunami of panic, bankruptcy, and social upheaval. Courageous action must be taken now to shut down Wall Street's operations. This does not have to await the outcome of endless legislative debates

Presidential authority, i.e., Executive Power to act in defense of the population, already exists within the constitutional office of the Presidency. As Roosevelt did, on March 6, 1933, when he declared a national bank holiday, a President can act today to shutter all of the financial gambling houses. This can be done with one stroke. There will be screams, gnashing of teeth and many vacant office buildings in lower Manhattan as the con-artists are sent to the unemployment lines. But the core of the commercial banking system, which will need to be broken up, reorganized and re-regulated, can and will be saved.

This action will then make possible additional moves to root out and crush all of the other practices of the British imperial financial system. Speculation, derivatives, and the like can be wiped out of existence. Many additional steps will have to be taken. For example, the New York stock markets will need to be radically changed, in the direction of returning them to the performance of a useful function, i.e., the capitalizing of companies to carry out productive expansion and research and development, rather than as the playground for get-rich-quick shysters. The details of how all of this is to be done are not important here. The absolute key to success is a ruthless war-time approach to victory. The Confederacy was defeated the day that Grant led his army across the Rapidan River.

It is also unnecessary here to discuss a detailed plan on what to do about the Federal Reserve System or what might replace it. The Federal Reserve has become so incestuously and pornographically intertwined with the practices of the bankrupt Wall Street speculators that its continued survival seems very unlikely. Obviously, some type of powerful national credit generating procedure must be established. Projects associated with a revived Space Program and U.S. participation in the World Land-Bridge must be given the highest priority in financing. We might need a national bank; there might also be several tiers of institutions for specific purposes, such as the specific role that the Asian Infrastructure Investment Bank plays today, that the *Kreditanstalt für Wiederaufbau* played in Germany, or that both the Reconstruction Finance Corporation and the Export-Import Bank played under FDR.

In truth, however, a rigid plan for financial "reform," down to specific details, is a criminally wrong focus. Only stupid people are preoccupied with such things. There is no mathematical formula for economic recovery. It comes down to human creative intervention. It comes down to willful intent. As stated above, in war, the first thing to do is to define your war-winning goals. That is the invariable.

Our goal is to crush the British Empire and to strategically reorient the United States from a trans-Atlantic orientation into partnership with the nations of Asia around commonly-held principles as to what is desirable for the future of humanity. That is the task.

If that is accomplished, in the context of the United States beginning full participation in the projects of the World Land-Bridge, while also establishing a partnership with China and other nations in space exploration, these actions will then define the necessary credit requirements and the nature of whatever needs to be created to fund these efforts. Simply figure out what we need to build, what we need to fund, and establish the institutions to accomplish that. It is only necessary that, whatever is done, it should cohere with the principles defined by Alexander Hamilton in his Four Reports.

Too much fuss is made about money. It is only money, a dead thing. The strategic re-orientation is what is indispensable. We must jettison all ties to the policies and practices of the London trans-Atlantic system. We must destroy the British Empire. We must join with the projects and mission that are coming out of Asia. Thus, we may save the American people, provide them with productive employment, and give them hope for the future.

To be crystal clear: If America fails to take these steps, we are doomed. We will go down with London and the rest of the trans-Atlantic system. Nothing will save us. Global war will become a likely certainty, sooner rather than later. The shift toward Asia must occur now.

III. Rise of Eurasia

Zepp-LaRouche Addresses Top-Level Conference in India

March 8—For close to three decades, Schiller Institute founder Helga Zepp-LaRouche has been the leading advocate worldwide for the policy of the Eurasian Landbridge, which she had originated with her husband Lyndon LaRouche. Her many trips to China on behalf of this policy in the 1990s, earned her the sobriquet there of the "Silk Road Lady."

More recently, the adoption of this policy by President Xi Jinping's China in 2013, under the name of the "Silk Road Economic Belt" and the "Maritime Silk Road," marked a turning-point in world history. This turning-point has been further consolidated by the far-reaching decisions of the BRICS nations (Brazil, Russia, India, China and South Africa) meeting in Brazil in 2014, and subsequent developments.

From March 1-3, Mrs. Zepp-LaRouche was a leading speaker and participant in the "Raisina Dialogue," hosted in New Delhi by the Indian Ministry of External Affairs and the Observer Research Foundation (ORF), in the first of what will be annual sessions. This conference, with over 600 guests from over 100 nations, focused on Asia's physical, economic, human, and digital connectivity, as well as the needed international partnerships to effectively address the challenges of this century.

The speakers included policy- and decision-makers, including cabinet ministers from various governments, high-level government officials, and policy practitioners, leading personalities from business and industry, and members of the strategic community, media, and academia. Among the inaugural speakers were the Ministers of Foreign Affairs from Bangladesh and India, Abdul Hassan Mahmood Ali and Sushma Swaraj; and

Under the leadership of the BRICS countries, a completely new set of relations among states is developing, based on mutual interest, economic cooperation, and collaboration in future-oriented, high-technology areas such as thermonuclear fusion, and space exploration and research.

several former Presidents: Hamid Karzai of Afghanistan, Chandrika Bandaranaike Kumaratunga of Sri Lanka, and Sir James Mancham, Founding President of the Seychelles. The conference was also addressed by Indian Foreign Secretary S. Jaishankar and several other Indian ministers, as well as former Chinese Foreign Minister Li Zhaoxing. Other speakers included Ding Guorong, Senior Vice President of the Silk Road Fund, as well as many other incumbent and former political office holders.

Mrs. Zepp-LaRouche addressed the first panel. She chose as her subject the urgent need for the extension of the New Silk Road into the Middle East, in order to guarantee the peace order expressed in the Feb 27 "cessation of hostilities" in Syria. Her message was very well-received. People came up individually to support what she said, including her interventions on other conference panels. Because this had been her first trip to India since 2008, numbers of Indians also approached her to warmly welcome her back.

The background to Helga's March mission to India features the efforts by British Empire agents in Washington and the European Union, to fragment the BRICS nations, including by pulling India away from the others. These include the efforts to impeach and prosecute Brazil's President Dilma Rouseff, as well as Obama's effort to overthrow the Jacob Zuma government of South Africa, which Zuma has attacked as another Washington "regime-change" operation. Among those trying to tempt India away from China and the other BRICS nations, was U.S. Admiral Harry Harris, head of the Pacific Command, who was also a speaker at the Raisina Dialogue.

The Crisis, the New Silk Road, And India's Role

by Helga Zepp-LaRouche

March 2—Helga Zepp-LaRouche, founder of the Schiller Institutes, spoke in New Delhi today at the annual Raisina Dialogue, co-sponsored by the Indian Ministry of External Affairs and the Observer Research Foundation, an independent public policy think tank based in India. The two-day conference is described by its organizers as being "designed to explore prospects and opportunities for Asian integration as well as Asia's integration with the larger world." The event hosted more than 100 speakers from over 100 countries. An edited transcript of Zepp-LaRouche's address follows.

Moderator: Now we have Mrs. Helga Zepp-LaRouche to speak on the Chinese Belt and Road initiative.... You have the floor.

Helga Zepp-LaRouche: Thank you very much. I want to thank the organizers of this very distinguished forum for giving me the opportunity to speak, because I think most people know that mankind is in one of its most severe crises, and perhaps the most important crisis in all of our history. The strategic situation is described by many analysts as more dangerous than during the height of the Cold War, at the time of the

EIRNS/Kasia Kruczkowski

Helga Zepp-LaRouche to Raisina Dialogue: The youth of India can be inspired "to take it as their own mission to participate in the economic transformation of Southwest Asia and Africa, and in this way, to be part of creating a future for all mankind."

Cuban Missile Crisis. The trans-Atlantic financial system is headed for a new crisis, worse than 2008, and the refugee crisis in Europe is really not only a tremendous humanitarian crisis, but it is about to explode the European Union.

The Crisis, the BRICS and the New Silk Road

Now, the question is, are we, as a human civilization, capable of changing wrong policies which have led to this crisis, or are we doomed to repeat the mistakes which have led, due to geopolitics, to two world wars in the Twentieth Century? But fortunately, we are also witnessing the emergence of a completely new paradigm. Under the leadership of the BRICS countries, a completely new set of relations among states is developing, based on mutual interest, economic cooperation, and collaboration in future-oriented, high-technology areas such as thermonuclear fusion, and space exploration and research, leading to a deeper understanding of the physical principles of our universe.

The Chinese New Silk Road program, One Belt, One Road, is offering a replication of the Chinese economic miracle to every country which wishes to cooperate in this win-win perspective. Already 65 states are participating in this new model of cooperation, and it is in the process of overcoming geopolitics, and thereby the source of war, potentially forever.

The new agreement between U.S. Secretary of State John Kerry and Russian Foreign Minister Sergey Lavrov for a ceasefire in Syria, is potentially a game-changer for the entire strategic situation, provided that especially Russia, China, and India immediately work with the countries of Southwest Asia to implement a comprehensive build-up program, not only for the war-torn countries of Syria, Iraq, and Afghanistan, but for the entire region from Afghanistan to the Mediterranean, from the Caucasus to the Persian Gulf. And with the trip of President Xi Jinping to the region—to Iran, Egypt, and Saudi Arabia—the extension of the Silk Road is now on the table.

The Schiller Institute published a 370-page study

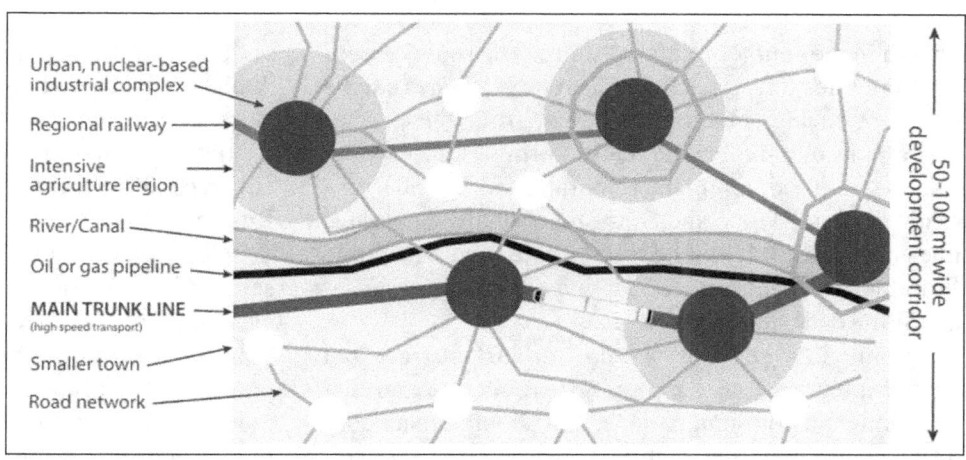

Urban, nuclear-based industrial complex
Regional railway
Intensive agriculture region
River/Canal
Oil or gas pipeline
MAIN TRUNK LINE (high speed transport)
Smaller town
Road network

50-100 mi wide development corridor

LaRouche PAC/lpac.co/silk-road

The Development Corridor concept. "This corridor should not just be rail, but should integrate transport, energy production and distribution, and communications, and should create conditions governing the location of new industrial development and new cities."

with the title, *The New Silk Road Becomes the World Land-Bridge*, which is already available in translation in Chinese, in Arabic, and soon in Korean, which is a blueprint for a comprehensive build-up of the whole world economy. It contains a very concrete plan for Southwest Asia. So this region, between Asia, Europe, and Africa, has a huge development potential, with great human and natural resources, and it is uniquely located.

The Five Seas strategy announced in 2004 by President Assad can still be a reference point for an infrastructure network between the Mediterranean, the Indian Ocean, the Red Sea, the Caspian Sea, and the Black Sea, making this region potentially a prosperous hub for vast increases in trade among Asia, Europe, and Africa.

Two Major Development Corridors

Two major development corridors, one east-west, and another one north-south, will not only include integrated fast train systems, highways, pipelines, water projects, industrial development, and agriculture. With modern technologies—such as nuclear energy for the desalination of vast amounts of ocean water and the ionization of moisture in the atmosphere—we can green the desert and reconquer large desert areas for agriculture and human habitation.

The New Silk Road, which already extends from Chongqing and Yiwu to Tehran, where the first Silk Road train arrived from Yiwu three weeks ago, can be extended from Tehran via Baghdad, Amman, and Aqaba, and then continue through a tunnel to Sharm el-

Sheikh in the southern Sinai to Cairo. The route crosses the Euphrates River, where ancient travel routes can be transformed into modern corridors, from the port of Basra in Iraq at the Persian Gulf, northwest to Aleppo. Existing railroads along the Euphrates in Iraq and a railroad between Aleppo and Deir ez-Zor on the Euphrates in eastern Syria, should be modernized, and a new line from there to Baghdad, connecting the main arteries of the Silk Road, should be built.

Again, this corridor should not just be rail, but should integrate transport, energy production and distribution, and communications, and should create conditions governing the location of new industrial development and new cities.

India's Role

A land route to India connecting the Iranian rail network to Zahedan on the Iran-Pakistan border, is on schedule to be completed. Other lines, for time reasons very briefly: from Deir ez-Zor to Tadmor-Palmyra to Damascus and Beirut; A north-south link from Syria to the industrial zones of the Suez Canal; a north-south railway from Damascus to Mecca and Medina; a tunnel under the Bab el-Mandeb Strait from Djibouti to the Arab Peninsula; and links to Europe, the Black Sea, and Russia.

India has good relations with practically all of the countries of the region and has already been asked by Russia and China to play a mediating role in such a developing perspective. As Prime Minister Modi has said, 65% of the Indian population is under 35 years of age, and that is the greatest asset of the country. These youth must not only be given a vision to increase the productivity of Indian agriculture—through the use of power, water, fertilizer, and high-variety seeds—so that the number of people working as farmers can be halved and that land be used for a build-up of infrastructure. But the youth of India can also be inspired to take it as their own mission to participate in the economic transformation of Southwest Asia and Africa, and in this way, to be part of creating a future for all mankind.

The realization of such a development perspective is the only way to end the refugee crisis and revive the economies of Europe and the United States, and to develop all of Asia. [applause]

IV. Noësis

A Dialogue with LaRouche on Leibniz and the Noëtic Process

Lyndon LaRouche discussed the process of noësis, creative thought, with the LaRouche PAC Policy Committee in a telephone conversation on March 2.

Dave Christie of Seattle: We have to operate from a global conception, and not have local operations. I think that's clear from some of the potential breakthroughs we've seen, and that there are more to come, given that there is nothing else on the table, in light of the dying British Empire. I am sure people have some general thoughts on where we are now and also where to go from here, so maybe we could just see what thoughts people have.

LaRouche: This would be mainly Leibniz coming

at you from details, and so that will lead to a broader element for discussion.

The Example of Leibniz

Ross: One of the key things to think about is the basis of the nation-state. Leibniz was not the first to do so, but he was a very,— the whole idea that was expressed in the American Revolution, and that was put into practice in that way, was that the goal of the nation-state goes beyond maintaining stability, and is outside of simply maintaining the power of those who already had it, but rather that the only justification for a ruler, or for law, was natural law—was developing the happiness of humankind, through our increasing understand-

LaRouche PAC

The LaRouche PAC Policy Committee in 2012. From left, Diane Sare, Lyndon LaRouche, Kesha Rogers, Bill Roberts, Rachel Brinkley, and Dave Christie. The dialogue presented here also includes Jason Ross and Mike Steger.

ing of nature to bring about an improvement in the lives of men and women.

I think that China is very clearly and directly doing that right now. I can just imagine what would Leibniz say today, if he could see the world situation. China has just pulled hundreds of millions of people out of poverty in about three decades. And on the scientific front, it is doing something totally new, going to the far side of the Moon.

Concerning the specifics of what I had to say about Leibniz this week, I just don't know how directly it applies to this discussion. It was about his time in Paris, and about the calculus, and about his legal work.

LaRouche: Yes. That comes from a whole series of things, especially from people who were creative figures, who brought things up to the point of Leibniz and into Leibniz's work. It's a process that you've got to see in that way as a totality, and I think we can illustrate what some of the steps are, which goes in a step-by-step kind of way, into what the prospects can be for mankind now, at the current time.

Ross: In terms of Leibniz's goals, consider what Paris was like when he arrived. This is the Paris of [Finance Minister Jean-Baptiste] Colbert; this is the Paris where the Royal Academy of Sciences had been set up. Colbert is pulling people together from around Europe to make advances. I think what Leibniz then did with that, was to put natural law into practice: He was very active in setting up academies—useful ones, not to study abstract and meaningless things, but to make the kinds of advances that would improve

Gottfried Wilhelm Leibniz, originator of the science of physical economy and inventor of the calculus (1646-1716). He saw the coherence between Christianity and Confucianism.

Jean-Baptiste Colbert
(1619-1683)

the economy, which his own work did—his own work on the windmills and the mines.

What he wanted to bring about in other nations—social improvement—was done through the academy, or through the common mission of developing new technologies and new sciences.

Obama's attack on NASA, this is a very direct attack on the mission of the nation. What's the point of having a nation if it's not doing things that advance mankind as a whole? It doesn't really have any justification to exist. That's the long-term purpose, the real purpose, of a nation or a society.

So, how do you develop relations among nations so that you are able to cooperate on that basis, towards things that make fundamentally new contributions? Obviously, working with China on these kinds of things, and that's a real basis for cooperation among nations.

Christie: Yes. Wasn't he two years old when the Treaty of Westphalia was signed? He was born in 1646. Of course that was the time of [Chief Minister Jules Raymond] Mazarin, in whose networks he was later to work. That environment, formed by this new conception of relations among nations for their mutual benefit, obviously has an echo for today in the "win-win" idea, which is really what Lyn has defined over the years, and is at the core of what Helga is doing around the Silk Road conception. I think of it as an environment which fosters creativity, when you have that kind of collaboration and relations among nations and peoples and cultures, in that spirit of mutual benefit. That becomes a real basis for a cultural renaissance.

Diane Sare of Manhattan: Consider what President Kennedy said, "Ask not what your country can do for you; ask what you can do for your country," and then what our nation can do for mankind. So he clearly had a much bigger view of mission than you hear from anybody today.

Broader Aspects of Discovery

LaRouche: That's pretty fair. That's fair. You can amplify that argument. Because it blossoms into a much larger, developing kind of element. You start with that, and then you say this leads to this, and this leads to this. And therefore you get a blossoming expression, a broader expression of what it all means, rather than just having a specific statement that this is a fact, this is a fact, this is a fact. You actually are tumbling into broader and broader aspects of discovery, and you, yourself, are hearing yourself speaking, and finding yourself saying things which are, to you, new. And that's the way that history often works, when it works well.

Rachel Brinkley of Boston: I was thinking of Leibniz when he got shorted in his legal studies; he was induced to be practical in his approach to schooling. And so he said, "Well, forget about it anyway, because my object is science. I'm not going to worry about this. I've got bigger pursuits of science." He hadn't even been trained in science so far in his life, but he had a sense that there is something that's knowable about the universe, and that mankind really had a lot of discoveries to make. He was really trying to figure that out on every level, how to get that to happen.

In language, he wanted to create a universal language, so that people could understand each other better; in religion, he said, "Look, everyone's going to be saved the same way," or something like that, "no matter what your religion." Yes, I think he definitely had the vision of what was needed to induce mankind to get to the next state.

Kesha Rogers and Mike Steger

LaRouche PAC

LaRouche: That's a fair description. But what do you translate that into? ... the point is that we make statements. We think the statements are correct statements, as such. But then you find out that there's something ahead of it, coming ahead, before what you're saying at that point. And you find that your very attempt to explain what you are proposing, impels you to make a statement which you had not intended at the moment that you actually gave the statement. Because you say something, you recognize that you've said it, but then you realize that what you've done is you've said more than what you thought you had intended to say. And you will, therefore rush in to try to add what you think is the thing that you had not explained or expressed. And therefore we actually, if we're functioning creatively, we're actually making discoveries faster, at a faster rate, than we ourselves can present these facts.

When people are really thinking, they are discovering something that they just said, but they hadn't known it before that time. That's the genius of this whole business, that when mankind is thinking, mankind has yet to think. Mankind has come to the verge of making a statement of discovery, and mankind *then, thereafter*, begins to discover what he was actually talking about!

Sare: I think that's one of the virtues of dialogue.

LaRouche: Precisely! It's the rich lode that you want to tap into, but sometimes you find yourself with an empty lode, but you wish you had found the lode. People start to say something, but then they stumble all over the place and say, "Forget it, forget it, forget it."

But when we have a flow of thought,— where actually it is thought, even though it may be stumbling,— the function of the human mind is to actually speak the future, before the tongue has left its perch.

Jason Ross and a colleague

LaRouche PAC

And look at what the space program was, in general, and I think we're not ignorant of the space program in general; we may have a lot of ignorance about the space program.

But, the point is, what we've learned from the space program especially, is that we have been able to understand the planets, distant planets and other bodies. We have become acquainted with these creations. And that teaches us that we can learn from the planets and objects in space. Because these things cause events which have not been anticipated, by word, heretofore, and therefore you are now compelled to use a new kind of word or a new kind of phrase, because you have to do that in order to describe the event that you're observing or studying.

You know, teachers often say, "these are the facts, you have to learn the facts." Well, that's kind of stupid because you know in point of fact that if it's important most of you have not understood it, haven't known what it was. And the fruit of the thing comes when someone has made a contribution which surprised, and as being legitimate, something which they had not known before.

So it's the ability to speak to the future, which is the point I would emphasize in this thing; the ability to speak the future, which is one of the things we learn from experiments in the space program. Just think about the first launching of man on the Moon, and this was the discovery of an object which had not been known until man landed on the Moon. So the space program was the voice of the future.

And you didn't want to get tied up with old stuff but you wanted to get more of the future, as new.

They Didn't Discover

Ross: The basis for the faith in an optimism about that being possible in the future doesn't come from experience. If you think about the optimism or the faith of Kepler or Leibniz, or Washington,— the sense of the possibility for victory or the possibility for discovery,— that doesn't come from looking at past experiences, although that can be part of it. That comes from a view of what is the universe like? What is the Creator like? What's the intent of this whole thing?

Brinkley: And I think the point about this sort of thinking of the future is that you're saying that every time you say something like that, it's going to be different and it's unique; you're not repeating something, and so it does have a power in itself just to speak like that, and you don't need an explanation to rely on for emphasis, but it's more the truthful quality.

LaRouche: Yes, it's the noëtic experience, in the literal sense of noëtic, that counts. Everything that really is useful....

And if you think about ignorant people, now there are two kinds of ignorant people. There are people who have different kinds of words they can use and multiply, but they can't think yet. All they can do is express something which occurred in their head at that point, but they had no actual discovery of the future. And the key thing here is, what we're talking about is the discovery of the future, that is, the actual experience of experiencing the future, in terms of an exploratory approach to a solution of knowledge.

And I get this when I do these things in Manhattan on Saturday afternoon. You often get people who try to argue from the past, that is, they will try to deduce a meaning of the future in terms applied to discussing the past. What happens is, then they get into an argument of one kind or another, and try to make a deductive appreciation of mere meaning of words as such. And that's where the problem comes in.

And the problem is, how do you get people to actually become scientists, in principle? Or, they make discoveries which are valid as a process of discovery, instead of trying to deduce the learning of words already used. Words as such and descriptions. How can you present a word, a name, a discussion point, which actually *lies in the future*? And the problem today is that very few people, especially professors, people of that type,— they are ignorant, because they don't know how to speak the future. They like to speak about *de*duction. Deduction, deduction, deduction; I deduce, I deduce, I deduce. You don't say "I discover."

Ross: It's better to have an addition than a deduction, huh?

LaRouche: [laughs] It can also be a crime, you know. Deduction can be a crime under certain circumstances. Especially when it comes from Obama.

Sare: I think this is the crucial shift in people's thinking we have to make, because if they look at the results of Super Tuesday and the elections as they're presented in the mainstream media,... everybody is going to do something suicidal or homicidal.

LaRouche: They don't discover! I had the discovery, years ago, of discovering discovery. And I found out that in that process that most people,— I'd take students or young people, professional people,— and I would find that they were emphatic in terms of what they said, what their opinion was, what their conclusion

Johannes Kepler
(1571-1630)

was; and you find out that they didn't know what the truth was, because they were simply trying to deduce an interpretation of the present and calling that the future. It's like the case of the bride who believes that her new mate is a turtle, shell and all. It's often a shell game, you know.

History, for most people today, historians, is a shell game. And you can look at Leibniz and others of the same temperament, and they always created something *new*. Therefore they had given something to the future, not something they'd given to the past, but something given to the future of mankind. That's what Leibniz did, entirely.

The Far Side of the Moon

Ross: It gives you a sense of the expertise or the knowledge that can come from having a strong intention. Leibniz wanted to develop the world, he wanted to develop mankind. And Rachel's bringing up his first studies in legal affairs, but he wanted to really be a scientist, and in a few years after arriving in Paris and really getting some scientific instruction, he's developed a whole new metaphor that totally changes the way we're able to talk scientifically about the relationship between causes and then the perceptual world, to make cause real, and that's what he does with the calculus.

So he wasn't a mathematical expert by any means, but he had an intention, and even in a field that wasn't his official strength at the time, he made a very significant breakthrough, because he had an intent that lay outside of that field itself, or trying to be an expert; he wanted to do something for mankind, and that drove him.

Michael Steger of San Francisco: It's also, you get the striving sense that he felt the responsibility to unfold the implications of what Kepler had discovered, which really makes what you're saying, Lyn, and Jason, so important. This discussion is so refreshing. Because it

Albert Einstein (1879-1955)

Library of Congress

really is the task: We have such remarkable potential in the world, and yet the present in the trans-Atlantic, it just makes me want to vomit. There's nothing here that you can rely upon. But we have such a potential,— but the question is can we actually bring it into existence. And you know that Leibniz truly fought to take what Kepler had discovered, and bring that into an actual sense of human society. That seems very similar to today, our challenge.

LaRouche: Well, you can see it from the back side of the Moon question: because at least so far we cannot be assured that we know what that experience is. So that's the kind of thing that makes everything meaningful, because you can locate the fact of an event, like the back side of the Moon. Mankind can speculate on what the back side of the Moon will show us, intellectually; that's a kind of discovery that's important. But I think what mankind really has to do is to become more used to devoting attention to those kinds of thoughts, rather than the conventional deductive methods. Deduction is defective, inherently. The very

fact, if you have a deductive method, you have shut off the future. Then you come up stumbling out with a guess, and you didn't know what you were talking about, but you came up and made a guess. And that kept your people amused, and then you went on to the next guess.

The fine art of science is something which very few people called scientists are capable of understanding, because they're talking about the past. They're trying to find the identity of the future in the past, and that's where the problem comes. These are the practical people, and the practical people are always in danger of death. Whereas those who have got the future, can live a little bit longer. Like Einstein. Einstein is a man who lived longer than he could live biologically.

Steger: It's foreseeable that we could be discussing Einstein's implications for hundreds of years, just given what we've seen, just so far with gravitational waves, and the whole organization of phenomena. Really, he's far beyond, even, maybe what we imagine.

LaRouche: People are so Earth-bound. And they can't get their mind out of the dirt.

Steger: That's why we call them dirty.

LaRouche: Dirty Bertie [chuckles]. Dirty Bertie and people like that.

It's very interesting to look at Einstein, today, looking at others earlier in history. The past is only interesting when it was in the process of creation.

Christie: You know, I was just thinking, that that's different than pedagogy, or I should say this: that pedagogy is, you could say that you're looking at a past discovery, but the recreation of a past discovery is always done from the standpoint of giving somebody an access to the means of discovery for future discovery. And that's very much different than the mode of deduction, which is not really oriented towards that, but is rather to take your fixed set of rules and apply that to all cases, and describe that somehow as a discovery, which, of course, it's not. It's not a discovery of new principle, but it's very different in pedagogy, because that's oriented, and oftentimes has created the very means of people creating pedagogical tools, examples, however you want to say it, is for the means of promoting the thinking capabilities of mankind. So, it's very much oriented towards the future.

Kesha: No Words for It

LaRouche: But also, we have lost the ability to discover the future. What happened is people can no longer understand the future. They don't. They may make fantasies, but they don't actually discover the future. And the educational system doesn't allow it. Popular opinion, formal practice in terms of the theoretical discussion,— it doesn't work. It doesn't work any more. There are very few people who do it. The Einstein case is exemplary in this thing. Einstein actually created the future, in his own mind. Almost no one, today, does that. Some people will fake something and say, "This is my discovery," but they didn't ever actually discover

Johann Sebastian Bach (1685-1750) at the Thomaskirche, Leipzig.

anything. But they're proud of this alleged discovery, and there was never a discovery made on that account.

And that's what gets me upset about our own organization. So many people in our own organization are so married to these kinds of prejudices, which are not worth anything, but they run around with "my story, my story, my insight, my genius," etc.,— but they don't know anything. And because society in general has not promoted the advancement of mankind's understanding of the future.

Kesha Rogers of Houston: You just provoked something. Because I was just thinking about the discussion we had with you prior to a webcast recently, after the breakthrough developments around gravitational waves. And you were making the point, which I think is relevant now, about the way people think about the universe and think about the Solar System is from the standpoint of a collection of objects in space, and that there's no coherence and no intention and no order to the world and

Conductor Wilhelm Furtwängler (1886-1954), drawn by Emil Orlik.

universe.

Megan and I went to an event where someone spoke on the gravitational waves breakthrough and the work that is being done on it. You had a sense that people were not thinking about this from the standpoint of the human mind coming to know the intention and order in the universe and that this was not something of the past, but was already Einstein acting upon the future and thinking about the future. People wanted to talk about it from the standpoint of different objects, or how it fit into their own understanding of the universe, or how their particular projects were going to be justified by it.

And listening to you now, I thought about this in terms of what you've always stressed on the question of music, particularly Bach, or [conductor Wilhelm] Furtwängler, the idea of thinking between the notes, that this is how the universe must be looked at. It's not a collection of objects, it's not a collection of notes, but it is what's actually shaping,— what is the unifying principle that's there, that's unseen, that's acting on the situation, that's between the notes. Then you have a better grasp of what is the future, that it is something that's not even explainable just in words. We try to talk about the breakthroughs that we're making and explain this to our contacts, and it's very difficult because you can't express it from just the words or the music in itself. But there is something happening there that goes completely beyond that.

There Is a Difference

LaRouche: Take the case of music. Take the case of music as you described. What's the problem? In the 19th Century, in the course of the 19th century, you had certain development. Then there was the point of going into the new century, what happened? What happened to music? What happened to poetry? What happened to everything? Everything was garbage! Popular music? Popular music of the 20th century and now, is garbage! And their opinion is, their idea of music is absolutely garbage. It has no reality whatsoever. It's trash. And people are looking for more and more exotic trash! They really are looking for something which is *new trash!*

That's what the problem is. The idea of the discovery of the future—the 20th Century does not allow the discovery of the future. They invent new sexes! Just think of the number of, the proliferation of new human sexes! They're all over the place. They invent new things. They actually invent new species and call them their lovers or something. It's like the man who married his turtle. He discovered a new personality. And it was only a shell game.

Sare: I think it's great; the work we've done with the *Messiah* so far, has shown people being able to recognize something better, even if they don't have it around them at all at present. You know, the two full houses that we got around Christmastime, and what we've got coming up. And the choral process overall has been expanding, among our offices. People are eager or able to recognize that there is something more

LaRouche: "What happened to music? Popular music of the 20th Century and now is garbage!" Musical culture was deliberately destroyed with the help of the Frankfurt School, not because music was the target as such, but because noësis was the target. Here, three of the Frankfurt School: Theodor Adorno (center) shakes hands with Max Horkheimer (left); Juergen Habermas is at the far right.

that should exist.

LaRouche: That's true. That's the difference. That *is* the difference. The fact of discovery which is a valid discovery, as a discovery, not a fake one. What the typical kind of entertainment does, it fakes something that never existed anyway. And as distinct from the discovery process,— take the case of Furtwängler for example. Furtwängler's work, particularly as he projected it in the later part of his life, more fully, and he had a complete understanding of what he was doing. Whereas the typical modernist has no brains at all. They make noises, but like turtles, rubbing with their whatever it is, they don't know anything,— they just do it. And so we really have a stupid population, in a sense. It's stupefied because it doesn't have any understanding of what the future is.

Steger: This discussion reminds me of what Elliot [Greenspan of Manhattan] raised last night. We had him give a short briefing on the upcoming conference. And this conception you're raising, and we've discussed now, seems to take what Elliot raised and that kind of process in a more universal way, which is what really can drive our political intervention at this point.

LaRouche: We can even do it with our own organization. We specify verified, presumed verified decisions, and we say those are practical decisions; and we nod our heads up and down and backwards and sidewards, looking at each other with different eyes and so forth and say, "Oh, yes, yes, yes, that's true." "Oh, yes, yes, yes, that's true." And none of it is actually true.

And the typical thing I get in our own organization is mostly what people say has no truth in it. [laughs] There's no thought in it. It's just junk, an ejection, like a turtle laying an egg.

Steger: Well, it's time we changed that!

LaRouche: Oh yes, good. [laughs] Yes, I think it should be changed.

Sare: We'll have the first rehearsal of our new Brooklyn chorus tonight.

LaRouche: Yes?

Sare: Yes. I don't know what to say about it. I don't know what's going to happen.

LaRouche: [laughs] Can you have a prescience of something? A difference between a known fact and a valid prescience? [Sare laughs]

It's like the egg just getting born. It's not quite the future, but it's nearly the future. And you're tempted to say, "Well is this the future or isn't it?" And when you get to that kind of perplexity, that's when you really are getting a delicious experience. Because you're being teased. When you're smug you know, you say, "I already know this." That's when you're stupid. But when you realize that you're on the edge of discovering something and you know it's not the present but it's the edge of the future, that's when you get the most intriguing kinds of experiences. Sometimes they'll torture you. You're on the edge of recognizing something as being true, but you can't quite prove it, but you're hanging up there, trying to prove that one way or the other, this thing has some meaning.

The Failed Trans-Atlantic System

Sare: Yes, it's a little ticklish right now.

LaRouche: (laughs) It depends how much fur you have.

Well, Leibniz, you know, is really very useful. If you can take all this stuff of Leibniz, you'll find it's all there. You just have to think of beginning with his father, and how he became independent of his father, and his father encouraged it.

Sare: I was thinking of another contrast between the general destruction of culture since 1900 and the receptiveness that we've been getting, and also economically, the rapidity of the rise of the Silk Road orientation, compared with the decades of the trans-Atlantic degeneration economically, and how quickly this thing is being taken up right now, and how more and more broadly it's being discussed. The potential, the future-orientation has to grab people. Well, if it didn't exist, we'd never change people, obviously. There's a receptiveness; there's something in humanity that responds to that. It is interesting how it's even spreading—even Germans looking at Syria, saying maybe we do need a Marshall Plan for this area, people being forced to acknowledge the need for physical economy. But still all of that, it's still in a different category than the Chinese who represent it at the highest degree right now, by doing something that's totally new, by going out there, going to the Moon.

LaRouche: Yes, what Ben [Deniston of the LaRouche PAC Science Team] has been doing in recent years, in this period, in his effort, as he goes out to explore the future, now, that's exactly what happens. You have to actually reach the future. And that's what China is doing; the Chinese development is one in that direction. And what you have now, what's happening with India right now, India's being tickled and provoked into doing the same thing that China has done.

On the other hand, you'll find the European system is one you can write off now, because the authorities, the people who are considered the authority, are essentially morally dead. Just think of people who are in finances or typical kinds of work. The codes of behavior in nations—the United States, France, Italy, and so forth—they're all scrapped. They have no validity for the future.

The important thing is to recognize that the area which we praise as the European system, generally, which we praise as the Americans, is not there! Most of it is a failure. It is simply a moral failure. And so we have to make this distinction—it's very important that we make the distinction between the future, the true future, which is like the back side of the Moon. The back side of the Moon is a very clear threat, that forces us recognize that there's something going on there which is not something ordinary.

Steger: Well I think we have that sense now.

LaRouche: [laughs] No, it's interesting. It's so

easy. You just take a nudge and you find yourself landing in an area which is a matter of truth, but you hadn't recognized it. The process of becoming—that was the secret of Leibniz. The process of becoming. We also had some other figures in history who had the same kind of quality.

Sare: A very becoming quality.

LaRouche: We have lots of friends with those qualities. Brunelleschi, for example. Now, the gentleman I'm looking at right now knows something about Brunelleschi, did some study, I think, two years ago, on the question of Brunelleschi. And I had a lot of time on Brunelleschi, and Brunelleschi had—

The Electress Sophia of Hanover, a protégé of Leibniz.

really no one in his lifetime knew what he was doing. Only after he had done it, did they begin to discover what he had done. And it wasn't just the architecture that was brilliant. But it wasn't *just* that. It was the whole idea of creativity. You know the idea of creativity in terms of the design of this temple that they created, and this design was absolutely unique, nothing like it had ever been done before. And he just did it! It changed everything.

And so, the creativity which he represented, Brunelleschi, was not easily replicated by any means. And this is what Leibniz worked on, exactly this. His own development to get closer and closer to this kind of intimate approach. In his last years of life, when he was working with the princess [Electress Sophie of Hannover], and trying to get the thing to work. And then she passed on and he passed on.

And mankind lost that connection. It had *no active connection*, to what they had represented. And mankind still has to wait, to find out and discover what had been possible back then. One has to recognize that Leibniz's life was terminated, willfully, by his enemies.

Self-Induced Death of the U.S.A.

Sare: And towards the end, they spent over a decade explicitly trying to make sure, and making sure, that he would never go to England. He would *not* be able to be

a force in the government there.

LaRouche: Yes! That was the whole ambition. That's what his last, concluding work was, exactly on that issue. And there was no one that could fill his shoes....

Anyway, I think there's room for rumination, to get some idea of what this is all about, what the issues are, what the blanks are in the process.

Steger: Hopefully not the blank stares. [laughter]

LaRouche: No. No, it's difficult you know. Our society is so rotten, in terms of culture, so empty, so sterile—and it doesn't smell good either. You just think about Wall Street, and you think about the members of Congress: What's the membership of the Congress? It's mostly a disaster, absolute disaster! The existence of the nation is almost a disaster. Its very existence. Most members of this society are killing themselves or being killed. In the usual kinds of ways: Taking drugs, negligence of various kinds, debilitation, intentional debilitation, all of this stuff is going on. We are actually watching the self-induced death of the nation of the United States! And you find the same thing is true, mostly of Europe, of most of Europe: It's dying. It's dying at an accelerating rate.

And the only area is in the Eurasian area, from that point on. Very little of society is worth anything. The British system of course is really mostly hopeless. It's either hopeless or desperate. I think the Britons, the best of them, are desperate. If they're sedate, they're stupid.

I think we have a mission. We have to concentrate on the Eurasian mission, because Europe, the trans-Atlantic community, doesn't function any more. It's collapsing. Maybe we can revive it, but right now, the culture which we're living in, in the United States, for example, and much of Europe, is *dying*; better said, *rotting*. And the idea of getting rid of that rotting process is the most urgent issue, I think, that we can consider.

Christie: Well, the Eurasian mission was the mission of Leibniz, too.

LaRouche: Yes, sure! But it was a period which was of that type. Various things happened to the United States. You had Leibniz, you had people who followed him, as leaders of the United States, but rare people, *rare*—very few. There were many people who were students of the United States development, but they were just that.

But with the arrival Bertrand Russell, of what happened at the beginning of the 20th Century, the 20th Century was a plunging of the entirety of the moral character of the United States. It was a plunge. And the plunge, except for the Franklin Roosevelt interval, was a disaster. I mean, we had a few great people, but they got assassinated; or something like that.

The United States is dying. The nation itself is *dying*, because we didn't do anything to keep it alive. Our opinions, our fantasies, our behavior in general, is degenerate. And we seem to be unable to get out of the habit of degeneracy. People dying of drugs, killing themselves. All the institutions are rotting away. This is our fine, old United States, and I don't know what we can do to save it.

And the Eurasian area is the proper center of reference for mankind today. There's not much left of the rest.

Hope in Eurasia

Bill Roberts: Lyn, I think this Kerry-Lavrov cease-fire deal does have a Treaty of Westphalia quality. If you look at the nature of how this came together, the question of who is wrong and who is right is actually secondary to creating the stability. In other words, the way the Russians set this up, is, "you come to the table, or you are going to be shot at." And so there's no toleration of people holding onto the past.

Now, that has to continue to develop in terms of what's the basis upon which this is going to evolve. But, do you think that, to the degree this actually has brought in an element of the United States, can we play this back into the United States?

LaRouche: Well, I would say that in my experience, going into the time that I was in service to the Reagan administration, I still had an optimistic outlook. Now, this is not an outlook simply of suspicion. But this was quite solid.

But what I saw with the arrival of the Bushes and Obama was entire British. In other words what destroyed the United States, what destroyed the Ameri-

cas,— and pretty much the Americas *have* been destroyed and most of Europe *has been* or is being self-destroyed ...

Forget it, the trans-Atlantic community, the trans-Atlantic is a lost cause, right now. It would have to be reborn. It will not come back to itself, it has to be reborn in a new form.

This is essentially the fragile,— still-fragile, but essential, Eurasian area. And the parts of the Eurasian area which are of some significance. And we in the United States are so proud of ourselves, that we pay no attention to the fact that we stink. Because we say, "well, it's my family smell." And it's getting riper, and riper, and riper.

Christie: Lyn, you look at this, and you see the moves in what Kerry's doing, and at one point fairly clearly stating, effectively, when a reporter asked him about Ashton Carter's objectives, saying, well, this is U.S. government policy. A clear acknowledgment, in fact, a break from Obama and his gang. So you see perhaps the potential of a resurgence of the institution of the Presidency coming in, to grab hold of, and contain Obama. But, in a normal time, if we had a functioning Presidential race in the 2016 election, and there was some sense of a coherent process around it, then could tie in the present functions of the institutions of the Presidency towards a potential role in the future, a Presidency that you could see as *really* being solid enough to box in Obama and what he represents. But because of this damned circus—and "circus" is a bad, and a limited term, it's a psychotic mess—I don't know how to describe it around these elections; there's just no coherence by which you could get a functioning institution of the Presidency. And it seems to me that the only way that you can actually get that, is by bringing what Russia, China, and India are doing, into the United States. I see the importance of the conference in April in that respect, but I just wondered if you have any thoughts on how to ...

LaRouche: I think the trans-Atlantic community is really in deep trouble. There are some things in Africa which are interesting, as promising, but I don't think there's anything in the trans-Atlantic community. Obviously, Australia's finished in the same way. Australia is degenerating in the same way.

And the only hope you get of any size, any substance, is in Eurasia. Everything else is rotted. The European system in the main is rotted. It cannot maintain itself, cannot sustain itself. The only thing we have is the Eurasian area, and there are problems there. But there is a hard core, typified by what Putin represents now, and by what China represents, and what India is coming back into, things like that. That's possible.

But the trans-Atlantic community which is, shall we say, the *remains*, of the decadence of the trans-Atlantic community, that's gone. Right now it's gone. In that form, it's gone. It would have to create a new form of society, such as the kinds of revolutions that have occurred in earlier parts of history in general. We've had periods,— of Charlemagne for example, things like that. You have very important figures who played key roles. *But!*— *but*, but, but ... that was what might have been.

And that's what we have to fight for: We have to fight for a future which is a true future. And I think the space program is probably the most nourishing suggestion to bring into consideration. That was the case, you know, originally with the space program. But when Obama, that son-of-a-bitch, as we call him, shut down the space program, the vitality and the possibility of the vitality of the United States was also assassinated.

Obama is a British agent, nothing but a British agent; a second-hand British agent, who killed a lot of people. And Hillary Clinton is one of the same make. She's a killer too, as has been explained recently. Poor Bill Clinton, he didn't know what he was getting.

Christie: Well, that's quite a lot. We could deliberate further on what we've discussed. We could reconvene at a later date. Unless you think ...

LaRouche: Ask him, he's right there!

Sare: That sounds good.

Christie: OK, well, the Maestro agrees.

LaRouche: Well, he does agree.... We can get some juice out of it.

Christie: It was fruitful, so we can get some juice out of it.

LaRouche: OK, pick your fruit.

Christie: Thanks, Lyn.

LaRouche: Have fun!